Your PIIGSty Guide to ECON101

A PIIGSty.com Publication

Darren Lawlor

© 2012 Darren Lawlor. All rights reserved.
ISBN 978-1-4716-2324-0

Table of Contents

1. **The Factors of Production (FOPs) and Economic Resources** 4
2. **The Producer** 5
3. **Economy of Scale** 6
4. **The Consumer** 9
5. **Markets** 10
6. **Demand** 11
7. **Supply** 13
8. **Market Equilbrium** 14
9. **Consumer and Producer Surplus** 16
10. **Price Elasticity of Demand (PED)** 17
11. **Cost Curves** 19
12. **Market Structures** 20
13. **Perfect Competition** 21
14. **Imperfect Competition** 22
15. **Oligopoly** 23
16. **Monopoly** 25
17. **Price Discrimination** 26
18. **Markets for the Factors of Production** 27
19. **Land and Rent** 28
20. **Labour (and Wages)** 29
21. **Capital (and Interest Rates)** 31
22. **Enterprise (and Profit)** 34
23. **Money and Banking** 35
24. **Measurement of National Income** 37
25. **Factors Affecting National Income** 39
26. **The Price Level (and Inflation)** 41
27. **Economic Objectives of the Government** 43
28. **Fiscal Policy** 44
29. **International Trade** 46
30. **Currencies and Exchange Rates** 48
31. **The Balance of Payments** 50
32. **The Evolution of the International Economic System** 52
33. **Economic Development and Growth** 53
34. **The Economics of Population** 56
35. **History of Economic Thought** 57

Introduction

To all readers

PIIGSty.com has always tried to be a beacon of clarity by providing a clear and comforting (even soothing) voice to those inquisitive economics students out there of every age, ability and ideology. You have told us what you want and we've made it our business to respond and make things that bit more simple for all of you and not just PIIGSty regulars!

As we're fond of saying, we at **PIIGSty.com** aim to cut through the rhetoric, jargon and nonsense to give our followers a well rounded but focused sense of how economics impacts their world (and as well all know, the subject ain't going away any time soon). Economics is an inexact and tricky science because (primarily) It's a social science. What that means it's a very fluid science. Economies are people after all. As you might expect, anything which is driven by people is very organic and changeable, and so is usually hard to pin down. Academics like to fudge the subject, padding out basic concepts by bringing in all these complex economic 'models' that do more harm to a students sanity than you'd imagine (believe me, I know!).

Your average citizen isn't an economist (lucky us). The average Joe and Joanna on the street leads their own unique and busy lives with their own private concerns and personal challenges. As a result, their actions don't often mirror perfect those rational but rigid economic models. Conforming is never fun after all.

A key cornerstone of economics is satisfying demand and we at **PIIGSty** have decided to ignore the others and do just that for our growing list of followers and readers. No longer will those hungry for answers to their economic questions be swamped under text heavy pages, get lost in boring tech-speak or be confused by drab monochromatic illustrations. This guide aims to satisfy your needs through 35 fully illustrated and colourful chapters distilled down into easy-to-digest chunks of simple but hearty goodness (your typical Irish stew).

So PIIGStiers, worldwide go forth, multiply (safely) and spread the word you've heard at the trough. Don't forget to bookmark (and read, if you wouldn't mind) the website, follow us on Twitter and watch out for more handy guides in the future.

Remember, your feedback is hugely important to us so log on to **PIIGSty.com** and comment on our posts, email us to say hello or, you know, just let us know how you're feeling. We'll listen.

Enjoy.

PIIGSty Editor
Darren Lawlor

1. The Factors of Production (FOPs) and Economic Resources

Factors of production are the resources of LAND, LABOUR, CAPITAL and ENTERPRISE used to produce goods and services

1 LAND
All **things supplied by nature** and **used in the production** of goods/services

i.e. farmland, forests, rivers, lakes, seas or minerals

2 LABOUR
All **human effort** which goes into the production of goods/services

3 CAPITAL
Anything **made by man** and **used to produce** goods/services

- **Fixed** stock of fixed assets i.e. buildings, factories, warehouses, vehicles
- **Social** owned by the community in general i.e. roads, water, sewerage
- **Working** manmade raw materials and partially finished goods

4 ENTERPRISE
Initiative involved in **organising land, labour and capital** and which bares the **risks** involved

The production of every good/service requires a certain combination of each **FOP**

Goods and services are produced **(supply)** to satisfy what people want **(demand)**

The interaction of **demand** and **supply** determines the **price (P)** people pay

2 Economic Fields

Microeconomics
(The Detail)

Its all about…FIRMS/INDIVIDUALS

The study of the behaviour and decisions of individuals and businesses in markets across the economy

Key Terms
Demand, Supply, Price Discrimination, Elasticity of Demand, Producer, Consumer, Market Equilibrium, Market Structure

Macroeconomics
(The General Picture)

Its all about the…wider ECONOMY

Deals with the structure, behaviour and changes in the wider economy at national, regional or global level

Key Terms
GDP, Interest Rates, Unemployment, National Income, Inflation, Exchange Rates, Fiscal/Monetary Policy

2. The Producer

The producers in an economy are firms/companies.
A **firm** is an individual unit of business which produces output and sells in the market

Sole Trader
A single person who sell a product/service on his/her own

Partnership
2-20 Individuals who share profits

Private Limited Company (Ltd)
Owned by **1-50** shareholders who have limited liability (only stand to lose what they've invested in the business)

Shares not traded on the stock exchange

Public Limited Company (PLC)
Owned by **at least 7** shareholders who have limited liability. Shares traded on stock exchange

Co-Op
Collective business loosely based around a product (usually agricultural such as butter)

Profit depends on a members volume of business

A firm aims to fulfil key goals

- Produce stuff **people want**
- Produce stuff at **prices people will pay**
- **Make profits** Organise production so revenue exceeds costs

How does a firm decide where to locate?

Nature of the Industry
- **Supply orientated?** Needs access to raw materials **i.e.** coal mines, oil wells, steel mills
- **Market orientated?** Needs direct access to market **i.e.** Apple stores in cities where incomes are higher and more people live
- **Footloose industries?** Flexible...depends on other factors **i.e.** airlines can move their planes and air routes to suit demand

Labour Availability
Certain skills vital and must be nearby i.e. hospitals locating near universities

Proximity to Similar Firms/Facilities
More efficient and less costly i.e. Silicon Valley hub for tech firms

Transport Availability
Firms might need access to International airports/subways/railways for their global employee/client reach

Energy/Telecommunications Availability
A firm might aim to be as environmentally friendly as possible *or* might want low energy costs, high broadband speeds etc

Government Policy
What is the government offering businesses? **i.e.** Availability of grants, corporate tax level, education policy on training potential workers

3. Economy of Scale

Definition: Factors which make it *cheaper* for larger companies to produce goods than smaller companies. This explains why some companies have cost advantages over others

Economies of Scale exist where average cost (AC) is declining

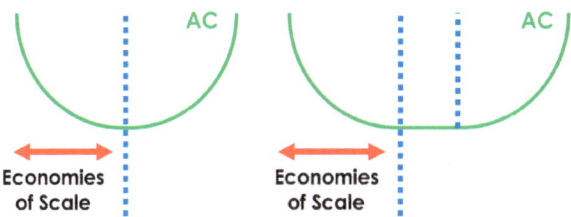

Definition

(A) Economies
Its all about costs!
Economies = Cost advantages/savings

(B) Scale
The amount of investment in fixed factors of production

Production Cost = Fixed Costs (FC) + Variable Costs (VC)

Total Cost = FC + VC
Average Cost = FC/Q + VC/Q

- VC/Q Depends on output
- FC/Q is the key! AC drops because of an increasing function of FC/Q i.e. better spread of fixed assets

Benefits of a Larger Organisation

Productive Efficiency
Lower prices
Consumers/Society Win

Competitive Advantage
Higher Profits
Company Wins

Short Run

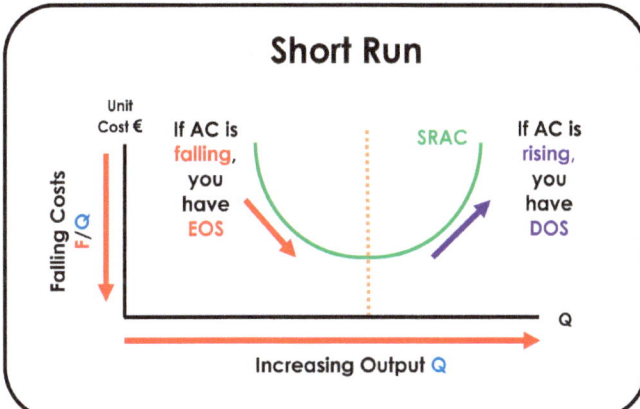

If AC is falling, you have EOS

If AC is rising, you have DOS

Long Run

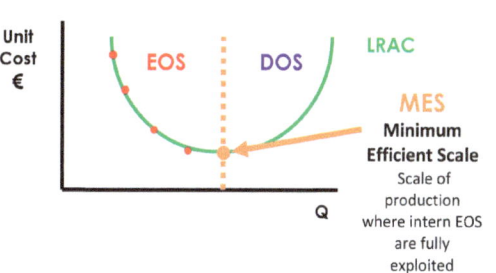

MES — Minimum Efficient Scale
Scale of production where intern EOS are fully exploited

Composed of an infinite number of firm sizes/scales i.e. many possible levels of production (combinations of SR cost and output that could be produced)

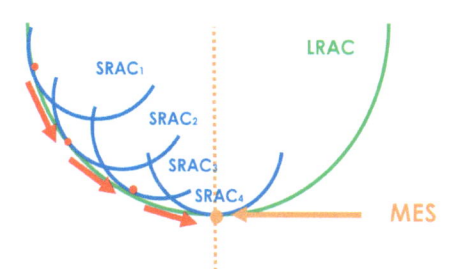

As the firm grows ($SRAC_1 \rightarrow SRAC_2 \rightarrow SRAC_3$), it will eventually arrive at the most efficient level of production ($SRAC_4$), where it produces at the lowest point on its AC curve. The firm has reached MES

Summary

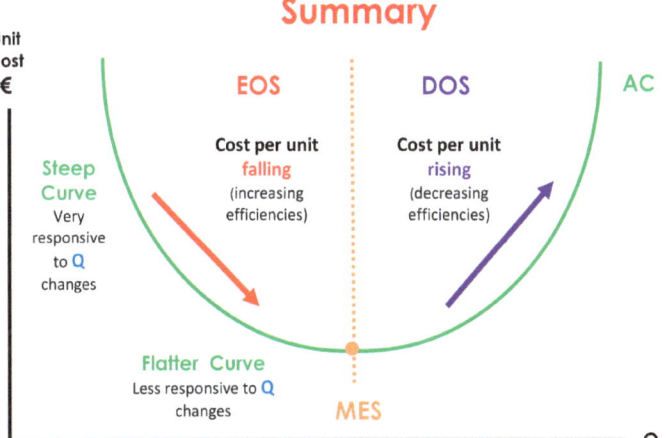

Steep Curve — Very responsive to Q changes

EOS — Cost per unit falling (increasing efficiencies)

DOS — Cost per unit rising (decreasing efficiencies)

Flatter Curve — Less responsive to Q changes

MES

There are two types of economies of scale: **internal** (streamlining processes within the company) and **external** (outside the company but common to all in the industry)

Example An industry with 10 firms; each firm produces 100 discs
Industry output is 1,000 discs. *Now imagine*....

Industry doubles in size (20 firms) and produces at the same level (100 discs). Industry grows so each firm costs may fall; efficiency gains per firm as a result of **resources controlled externally** to the firm

Exhibits **External** EOS
Every firm benefits

Industry output remains the same (1,000 discs). Numbers of firms in the industry falls (to 5 firms) that each of the remaining firms produce 200 discs. If costs of production remain the same, advantage goes to large firms

Exhibits **Internal** EOS
Larger firms benefit

Internal Economies of Scale

Technical
- Buy/utilise better machinery/methods
- Promotion of integrated production
- Specialisation of labour
- Learning by doing principles (realise best production methods and tech)

Managerial/Labour
- Bargaining power with employees
- Use new financial resources to outsource unnecessary elements
- New mechanical process = 'human error' risks/costs removed

Commercial
- **Marketing** Spread of advertising costs over wider output
- **Monopsony** Bulk buying @ discounted prices

Financial
- Better access to credit
- Larger = potential of quote on stock exchange = cheaper borrowing

Network
- Perfect for mainly online companies (cheap expansion)
- eCommerce success

Risk Bearing
- Firms diversify product portfolio to reduce risk
- Many 'back-up' products and materials/parts
- Production can shift according to demand

Internal Diseconomies of Scale

Technical
- **Repetition** as a result of specialisation. Management layers grow unwieldy
- **Duplication**
- **Monitoring costs** (time)

Managerial/Labour
- **Communication** (due to no. of workers)
- Issue of **non-productive workers**
- Issue of insuring against **fidelity** (employee dishonesty/stealing)
- **Conflict/Absenteeism/Morale** 'merely cogs in the production machine'

Financial
- **Overreliance on cheap credit** for expansion
- Risk of **bad debts**

External Economies of Scale

Infrastructure
- Better transport network
- Airports/Ports/Motorways/ Local roads
- Cheaper/More direct access to raw materials

R&D Facilities
- Local universities/ Institutes
- Availability of training courses/colleges

Component Economies
- Relocation of component suppliers
- Relocation of support businesses
- Growth of 'industrial parks/estates' i.e. Shannon Free Zone, Canary Wharf, Silicon Valley, IFSC Dublin

External Diseconomies of Scale

Infrastructure
- Overuse causing damage, congestion, high accident rate

Labour
- Demand for skilled labour explodes – skills needed in short supply = hiring of less qualified
- Hits productivity

Overexploitation
- Raw materials demand rises = price rises
- Usage of lower quality materials! Risky

Economies of Scale

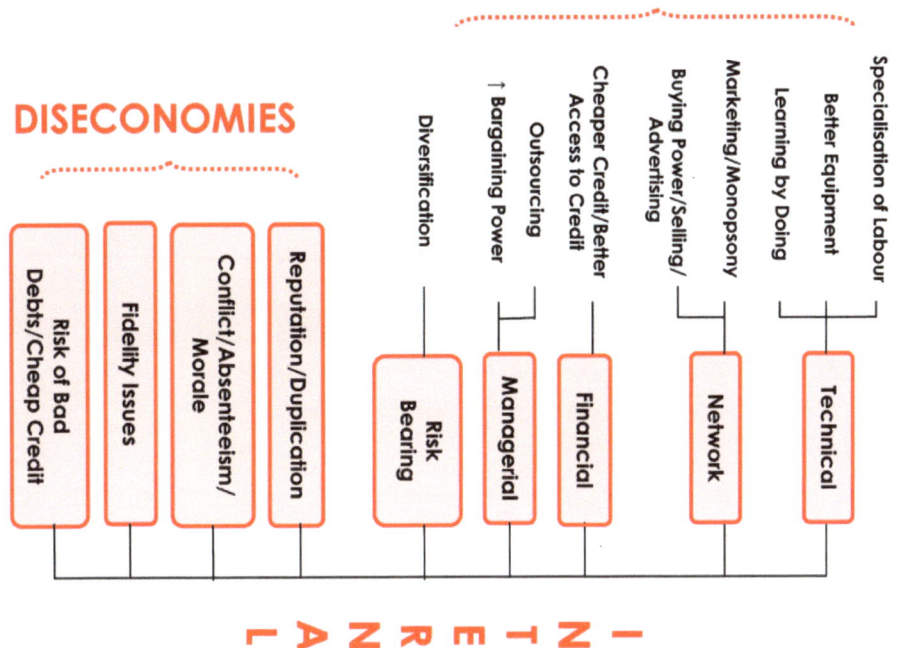

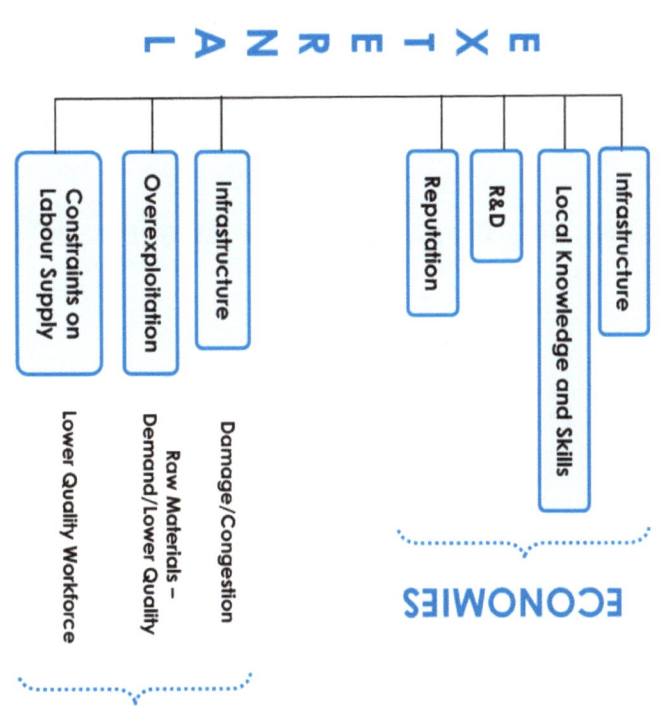

4. The Consumer

A **consumer** is a decision making unit that buys goods/services (g/s)
Assumptions are made in relation to human/consumer behaviour…

Income — Our ability to buy g/s depends on **income** and this is **finite** (it has a limit **i.e.** our weekly/monthly wages)

Choice — As our incomes are **finite**, once our basic needs are met (food, shelter and warmth) the 'excess' income becomes *disposable* income. We spend this freely as we choose. What will we choose?

Rationality — People will spend income to maximise their own satisfaction (utility)

An **Economic Good** has **3** characteristics…

Economic Good

- **PRICE** — The good must be scarce in relation to demand (producing infinite amounts of it would mean selling each for very little)
- **UTILITY** — Satisfaction is key otherwise why would you want it?
- **TRANSFERRABLE** — Can physically pass person to person

Law: As more units of a good are consumed, satisfaction per unit falls (you become bored/full). But how do know this 'law' exists?

Law of Diminishing Marginal Utility

- **DISCOUNTS** — It exists because stores offer discounts encouraging people to buy more at a lower price per unit
- **HUMAN LIMIT** — We all know we have physical limits to what we can eat or drink
- **EXCEPTIONS** — Addiction drugs such as alcohol, nicotine or medicines/ prescription drugs

So, why do consumers buy certain goods/services?

FUNCTIONAL Demand
Buying a g/s to do a specific task
Example Hammer, paint, car part etc

BANDWAGON /FAD Effect
Buying a g/s to be part of a trend
Example Clothes, new Tech products

EXCLUSIVE Demand
Buying expensive goods with status to them
Example BMW, 5* Hotel stay, iPhone

SPECULATIVE Demand
Buying a g/s now because you think the price will rise in the future
Example Housing

IMPULSE Buying
Spur of moment [purchase, well positioned in the supermarket (**good merchandising**) or because of a good ad campaign (**good marketing**)

5. Markets

A **market** is all Individuals/companies involved in buying *or* selling a good or service

Questions

- **DEMAND** — **Quantity** Consumers willing to buy at different prices
- **What** Should We Produce?
- **Who** Are we doing it for?
- **How** Will We Make it?
- **Rewards** For the suppliers of the FOPs?
- **SUPPLY** — **Quantity** Producers willing to make available at different prices

4 Types of Markets

1. Factor Market

Where a Factor of Production (FOP) is bought or sold

Buyer = Entrepreneur

Use = Production of Goods and Services

Seller = Owner of the FOP i.e. we all sell our labour for wages/salary

2. Intermediate Market

Where an output is sold as a raw material (i.e. iron) and used an input to produce another good (i.e. steel)

Intermediate goods aka 'Producer goods'

3. Final Market

Consists of Goods/Services which are complete, provide consumer utility and they are prepared to pay a price

Final market goods aka 'Consumer goods'

4. Foreign Exchange Market

Where currencies are bought/sold for profit. This facilitates international trade between nations with different currencies

Price = exchange rate

6. Demand

Movement Along Demand Curve

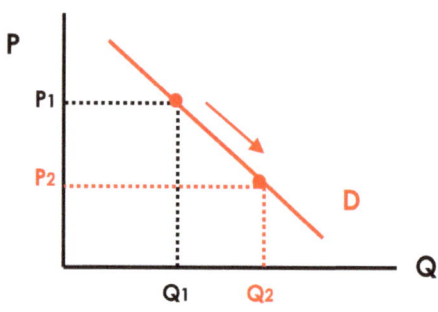

Caused By: A Change in Price

Demand Curve Shifts

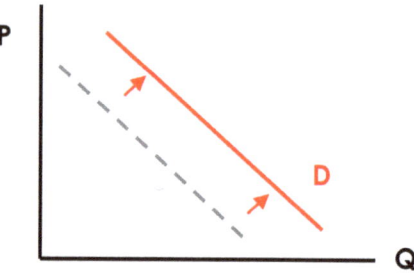

Caused By: A Change in Demand

What 6 factors affect Demand?

$$D_x = f(P_x, P_c, P_s, y, t, E)$$

Demand for Good X (D_x) depends on:
1. The Price of Good X (P_x)
2. The Price of Complementary Goods (P_c)
3. The Price of Substitute Goods (P_s)
4. Income (y)
5. Taste (t)
6. Future Expectations (E)

Basic Law of Demand: ↑Price P ↓Quantity Demanded Q_D and ↓P ↑Q_D

There are some *exceptions* to this…

Giffen Goods (GGs)	Snob 'Status Symbol' Goods	Expectation/ Speculative Goods
Necessity goods i.e. bread, milk. If the price of GGs goes up, more income is spent on GGs than luxuries, raising the Q_D	Show of wealth/success in goods means you will spend more to be part of an exclusive trend	i.e. property Buy now as you might expect price next year to be unaffordable

- **Complementary Goods:** Two goods which require the use of another i.e. tea and milk, bread and butter, printers and ink cartridges
- **Substitute Goods:** Goods with similar characteristics and used in identical ways i.e. Aldi Cornflakes V. Kellogg's, different brands of bread, milk, butter, chocolate etc

2 different types of income…

a) **Money Income** – nominal earnings expressed as wages/salary
b) **Real Income** – purchasing power of earnings (what you can buy)

NORMAL GOOD	INFERIOR GOOD
Good with positive income effect	Good with negative income effect
More Y = More Q_D	More Y = Less Q_D
Less Y = Less Q_D	Less Y = More Q_D

It is possible to get a rise in **money income** and suffer a decline in **real income** as cost of living (groceries, transport costs etc) might exceed rise in actual money

For all goods if consumer tastes react *positively* toward them…**more** will be demanded. If tastes change *negatively* toward a good…**less** will be demanded

Expectations change depending on (1) Future Price (2) Future availability (3) Future Income

We can tell one type of good from another with
3 simple tests on any test 'good/service'

INCOME EFFECT	SUBSITITUTION EFFECT	PRICE EFFECT
What effect does a rise/drop in income have on demand for the good?	What effect does a rise/drop in the price of a substitute good have on demand?	What effect does a rise/drop in the price of the good itself have on demand?

Good	Income Effect	Substitution Effect	Price Effect	Type
A	More	More	More	Normal Good
B	**Less**	More	More	Inferior Good (Not Giffen Good)
C	**Less**	More	**Less**	Inferior Good (Also Giffen Good)

Remember: ALL giffen goods are inferior goods but **not** all inferior goods are giffen goods

7. Supply

Basic Supply Curve

Basic Law of Supply
↑Price P ↑Quantity Supplied Q_s
and ↑P ↑Q_s

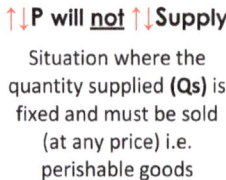

Perfectly Inelastic Supply

↑↓P will **not** ↑↓Supply

Situation where the quantity supplied (Qs) is fixed and must be sold (at any price) i.e. perishable goods

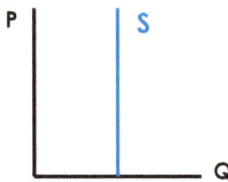

Minimum Supply

A **minimum price** (P_1) is established by suppliers below which **supply = 0** i.e. Trade Union imposing minimum price at which workers will be supplied

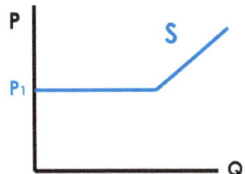

Maximum Output (Limited Capacity)

A point is reach where more **cannot be supplied (Q_1).** Producers cannot increase output due to constraints in their factory, i.e. lack of inputs i.e. machinery, raw materials

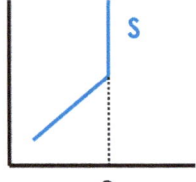

What 5 Factors Affect Supply?

$$S_x = f(P_x, P_r, C, T, U)$$

Supply of Good X (S_x) depends on:

1. The Price of Good X (P_x)
2. The Price of Related Goods (P_r)
3. Cost of Production (**C**)
4. State of Technology (**T**)
5. Unforeseen Circumstances i.e. adverse weather (**U**)

P_x — Basic Law of Supply: ↑Price P ↑Quantity Supplied Q_s and ↓P ↓Q_s

P_r — **Related Goods** are goods which could be produced instead of **Good X**. If the price of a related good (P_r) rises, the supplier will shift production away from **Good X** and increase the supply of **Good R** will rise at the expense of **Good X**

C —
SUPPLY FALLS if...	SUPPLY RISES if...
• Labour costs *rise*	• Labour costs *fall*
• Raw material (input) costs *rise*	• Raw material (input) costs *fall*
• Taxes *rise*	• Taxes *fall*
• Grants/Subsidies to firms *fall*	• Grants/Subsidies to firms *rise*

T — As technology **improves**, supplying (distributing) goods becomes easier and less costly

U — Factors outside the control of the firm might jeopardise shipments i.e. warehouse fire, transport difficulties due to adverse weather or war

8. Market Equilibrium

We can summarise what determines changes in
demand and supply as follows:

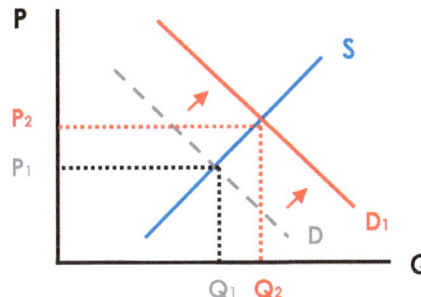

RISE IN DEMAND

1. ↑P_S Price of substitute good
2. ↓P_C Price of complementary good
3. ↑Y Income (normal good)
4. Change in Tastes (t) in favour of good
5. Expectations (E) of future scarcity and price rise

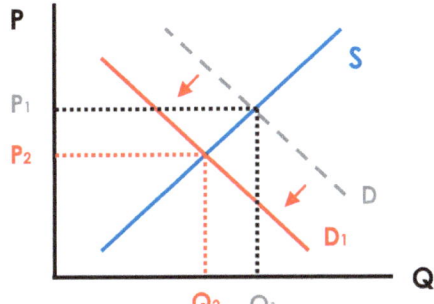

FALL IN DEMAND

1. ↓P_S Price of substitute good
2. ↑P_C Price of complementary good
3. ↓Y Income (normal good)
4. Change in Tastes (t) against good
5. Expectations (E) of future abundance and price fall

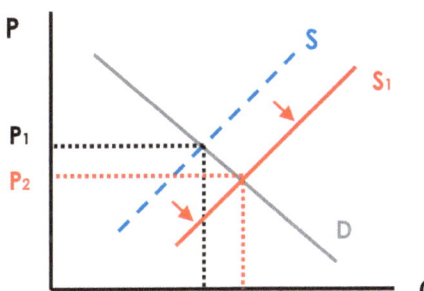

RISE IN SUPPLY

1. ↓P_R Price of related good
2. ↓C Cost of production
3. ↑T State of technology
4. Favourable unplanned factors (i.e. good growing conditions for crops)

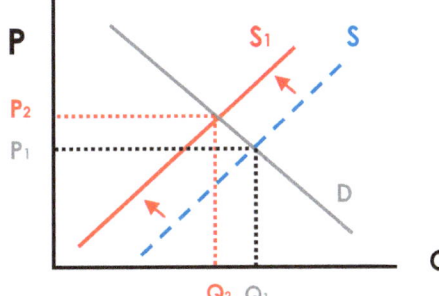

FALL IN SUPPLY

1. ↑P_R Price of related good
2. ↑C Cost of production
3. Unfavourable unplanned factors (i.e. severe growing conditions for crops)

KEY: The interaction of **supply** and **demand** determines the optimal **PRICE** and **QUANTITY DEMANDED** (aka Equilibrium P and Q)

So, what changes the **equilibrium price** and **equilibrium quantity**?

Looking at these graphs...

Change	Equilibrium Price	Equilibrium Quantity
Demand Rises	Rises	Rises
Demand Falls	Falls	Falls
Supply Rises	Falls	Rises
Supply Falls	Rises	Falls

The Interaction of Demand and Supply

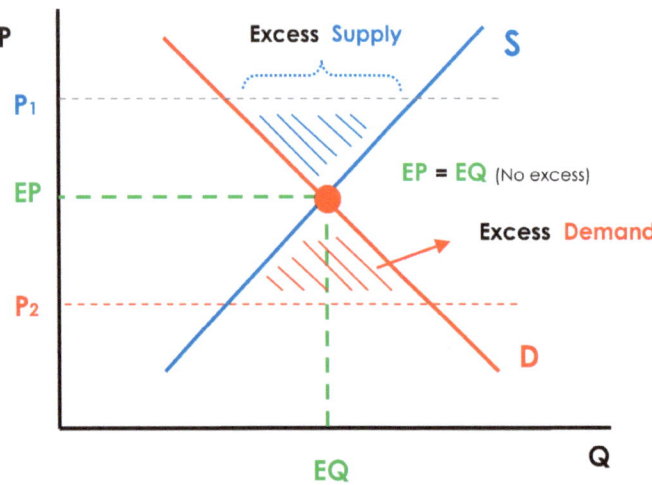

9. Consumer and Producer Surplus

Price is determined by the interaction of demand and supply. But we don't always pay the maximum price that we are willing to pay…often we get a bargain!

Its all about value (for consumers) and cost (for producers)

Value of one more unit of a good/service is its marginal (extra) benefit (MB). This 'willingness to pay' determines demand

Demand curve = MB curve

When consumers buy something for **less than its worth** to them, they receive a consumer surplus

Cost of producing one more unit of a good/service is its marginal (extra) cost (MC). This 'willingness to produce' determines supply

Supply curve = MC curve

When producers supply something for more than the **marginal cost of production**, they receive a producer surplus

Consumer Surplus

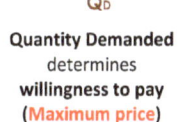

Price (P) determines Quantity Demanded
@P, Q_D is demanded

Quantity Demanded determines willingness to pay
(Maximum price)

Producer Surplus

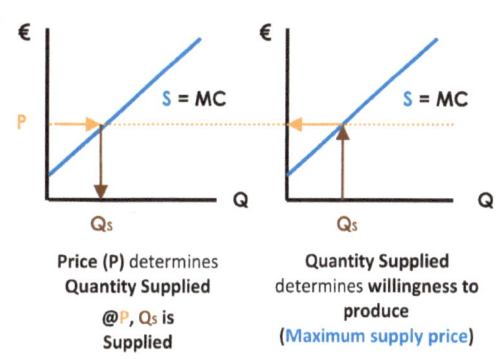

Price (P) determines Quantity Supplied
@P, Q_S is Supplied

Quantity Supplied determines willingness to produce
(Maximum supply price)

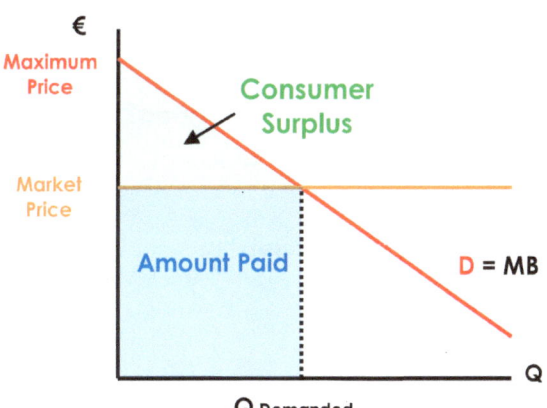

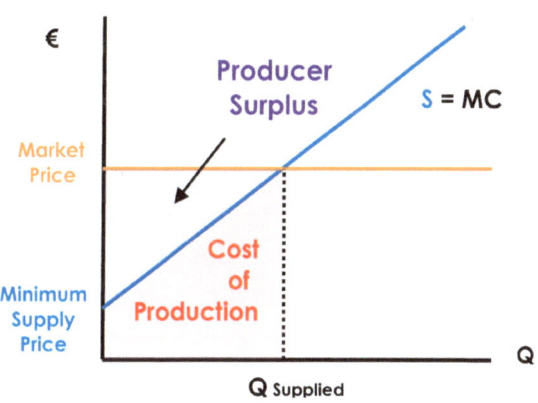

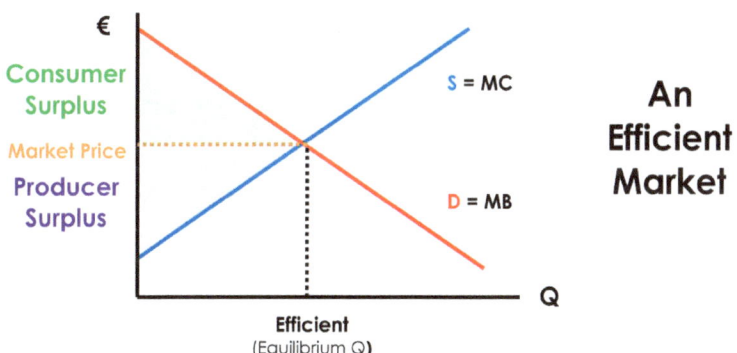

An Efficient Market

16

10. Price Elasticity of Demand (PED)

As you saw in #8, sometimes to reach equilibrium P and Q, demand and supply have to adjust - this takes <u>time</u>

Sometimes, demand changes very **quickly** in response to price changes – demand is price **elastic**
Sometimes, demand changes very **slowly** in response to price changes – demand is price **inelastic**

Price Elastic Your mobile phone provider **increases** its charges – you can switch to a choice of other companies *or* you can cut your usage to fit the new tariff

Price Inelastic When oil prices **rise**, you can't change suppliers – you have to just pay the higher price. Some might choose to drive less or buy less heating oil but demand stays relatively stable

How to Measure PED?

$$PED = \frac{\%\Delta Q}{\%\Delta P} \quad \text{or} \quad \frac{\text{Proportionate Change in } Q_D}{\text{Proportionate Change in } P}$$

P_1 = Original Price Q_1 = Original Quantity Demanded
P_2 = New Price Q_2 = New Quantity Demanded

Is a good a normal good?
<u>Ans</u>: PED must be **negative**

$$PED = \frac{\%\Delta Q}{\%\Delta P} = \text{- or + value (decimal answer)}$$

$\downarrow Q_D$ = MINUS or $\uparrow Q_D$ = PLUS
$\uparrow P$ PLUS $\downarrow P$ MINUS

Both **NEGATIVE**

Exceptions
Not **ALL** goods obey the Law and Demand (*See* #6)
- Inferior Goods
- Giffen Goods
- Snob 'Status Symbol' Goods

All these have a **POSITIVE** PED

Working Out the Sums...

1 PERFECTLY INELASTIC
PED = 0
Q_D isn't changed by a Δ in P
Vertical Demand Curve

2 PRICE INELASTIC
PED < 1
Q_D isn't very responsive to Δ in P
If P↑10% and Q_D↓ 2.5%
PED = 0.25

3 UNIT ELASTIC
PED = 1
Q_D is perfectly responsive to Δ in P
If P↑10% and Q_D↓ 10%
PED = 1

4 PRICE ELASTIC
PED > 1
Q_D is responsive to Δ in P
If P↓5% and Q_D↓ 10%
PED = 2.0

5 PERFECTLY ELASTIC
PED = ∞
Q_D falls to zero after any Δ in P
Evident in perfectly competitive markets

What Determines PED of a good?

1. **Availability of Substitutes**
   - > No. of substitutes
   - > Price elasticity
2. **Its Price (Luxury or Necessity)**
   - > Price >Likelihood the good is **elastic** (a price rise could be too much for current customers)
3. **Durability**
   - > Price could mean postponing replacing the good (i.e. washing machines) – **price elastic**
4. **Income Spent**
   - A low proportion of income spend on it means its more likely to be **price inelastic**
5. **Brand Loyalty/Habits**
   - If strong loyalty/addiction, you will buy at any price = **price inelastic**
6. **Complementary Good?**
   - If its 1 of 2 goods used together cheaper good = **price inelastic**

Price Elasticity of Demand (PED) for Normal Goods

1 PERFECTLY INELASTIC DEMAND

- A good is have perfectly inelastic demand if a change in its price (**P**) will cause **no** change in the **Q**$_D$
- Demand is fixed, **Q**$_D$ wont change
- **Maximise Revenue/Profit** by increasing **P** as much as possible. Costs wont rise as **P** does because no more goods are produced
- **Example:** Lifesaving drugs

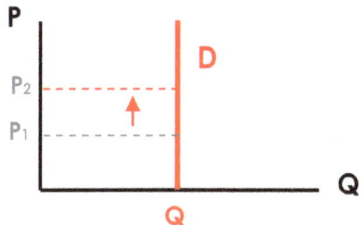

2 RELATIVELY INELASTIC DEMAND

- An increase from **P1** to **P2** will cause a smaller drop in **Q**$_D$ from **Q1** to **Q2**
- Demand is not very responsive to P changes
- **Example:** Petrol, Alcohol, tobacco (*Less* responsive – *more* likely to be taxed)

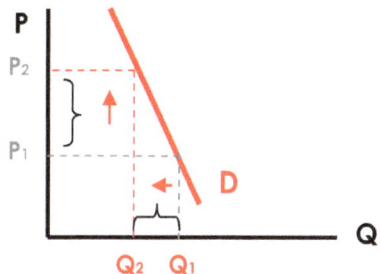

3 UNIT ELASTICITY OF DEMAND

- If the prop change in **Q**$_D$ = prop change in **P** (i.e. **PED=1**)
- **Revenue** = Constant
- **Profit** = Max profit by increasing **P** as high as possible – could sell sell at higher **P** (less costs/unit more profitable)

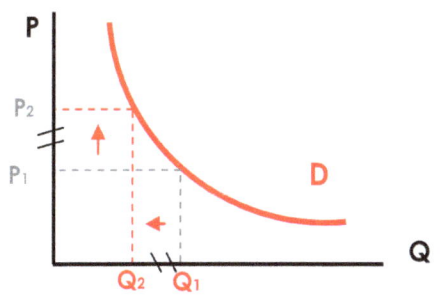

4 RELATIVELY ELASTIC DEMAND

- If proportional change in **Q**$_D$ is greater than proportional change in **P** = Good is elastic
- Demand for such goods is **very responsive** to **P**

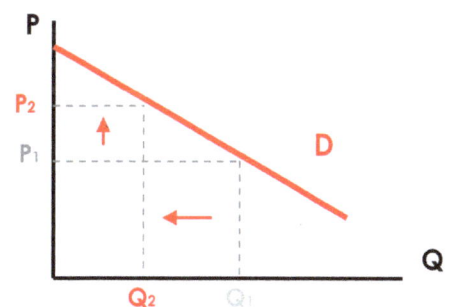

5 PERFECTLY ELASTIC DEMAND

- Situation where **PED = ∞**
- Customers are prepared to buy ALL they can of a product at **ONE price ONLY**
- Any increase in **P** will cause demand to fall to 0
- **Example:** Any homogenous product with many substitutes i.e. potatoes, vegetables

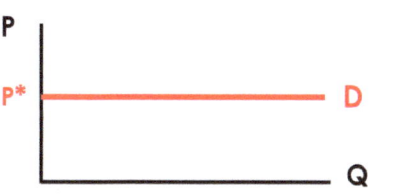

11. Cost Curves

A cost curve is a graph of the costs of producing a good as a function of the amount of that good produced. Firms will always aim to minimise costs per unit while maximising profits (revenue *less* costs)

The Marginal Cost Curve
(Think of firms cost of producing apples...)

TinyApple Inc makes only 5 apples

- Each of the 5 apples costs €1 each to produce so the average cost (AC) = **€1**
- The firm decides to make one more apple (marginal cost MC = the cost of that *extra* apple)
- The extra/marginal cost is **80c**

80c < €1   so   **MC < AC**

- Now, 6 apples are produced costing €1, €1, €1, €1, €1 and 80c...average **97c each**

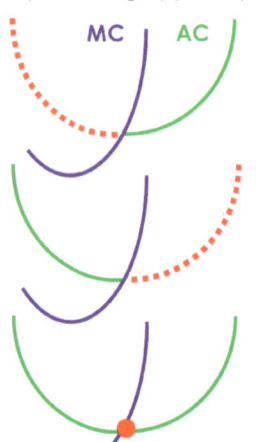

If **MC<AC**...then **AC** is **FALLING**

If **MC>AC**...then **AC** is **RISING**

If **MC=AC**...then **AC** is **at its lowest point**

The Average Cost Curve

AC (downward) ... AC (upward)

Downward sloping
1. Better spread of fixed assets
2. Specialisation of labour

Upward sloping
Diseconomies of scale

MES: Minimum Efficient Scale
Scale of production where internal **Economies of Scale (EOS)** are fully exploited

The Revenue Curves

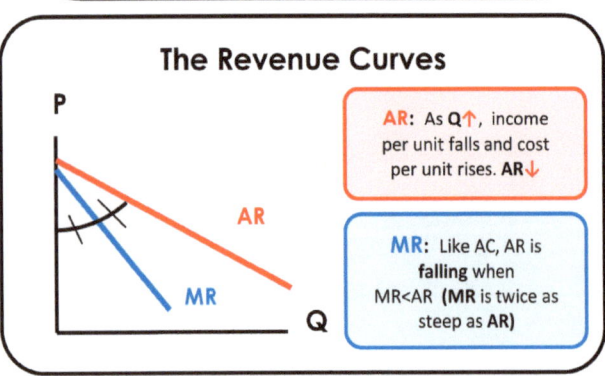

AR: As Q↑, income per unit falls and cost per unit rises. **AR↓**

MR: Like AC, AR is **falling** when MR<AR **(MR is twice as steep as AR)**

More Cost Curves

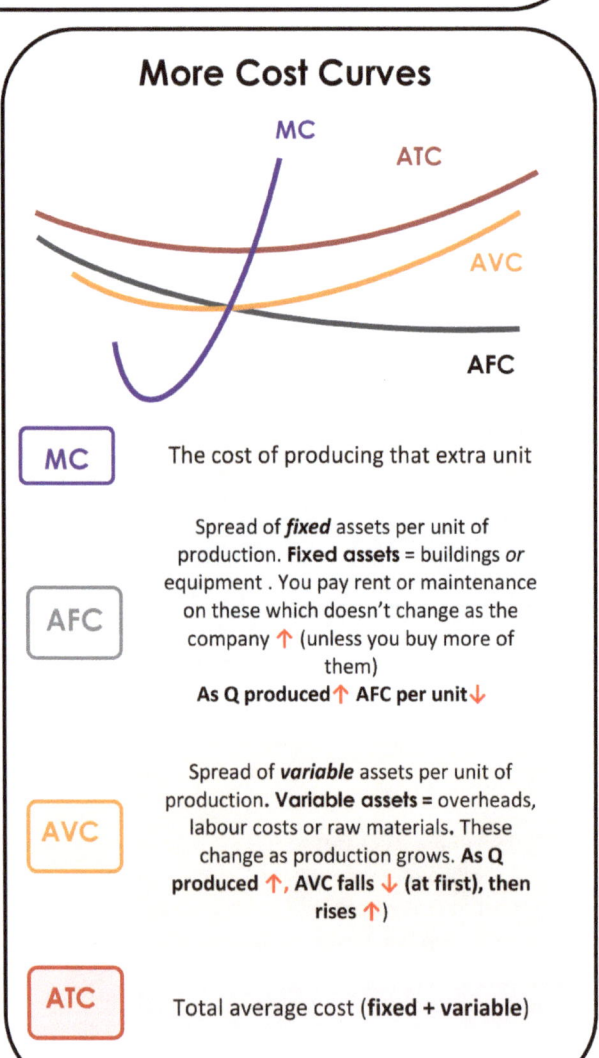

MC — The cost of producing that extra unit

AFC — Spread of *fixed* assets per unit of production. **Fixed assets** = buildings *or* equipment. You pay rent or maintenance on these which doesn't change as the company ↑ (unless you buy more of them)
As Q produced ↑ AFC per unit ↓

AVC — Spread of *variable* assets per unit of production. **Variable assets** = overheads, labour costs or raw materials. These change as production grows. **As Q produced ↑, AVC falls ↓ (at first), then rises ↑)**

ATC — Total average cost (**fixed + variable**)

12. Market Structures

There are **4 different types** of market structure

Perfect Competition → Imperfect Competition → Oligopoly → Monopoly

Increasing market power, concentration and market price
Declining market efficiency and competition

Short Run (SR) | Long Run (LR)

Perfect Competition

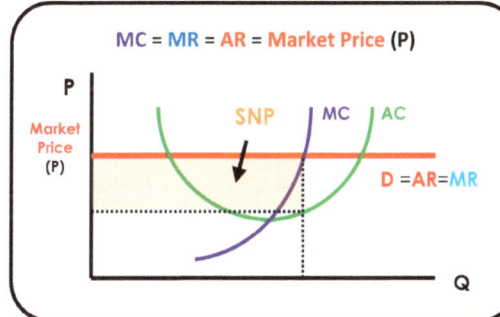

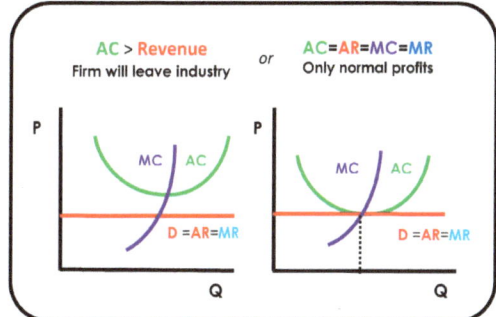

Imperfect Competition

SAME AS MONOPOLY

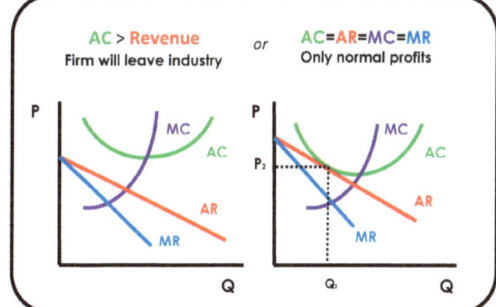

Oligopoly

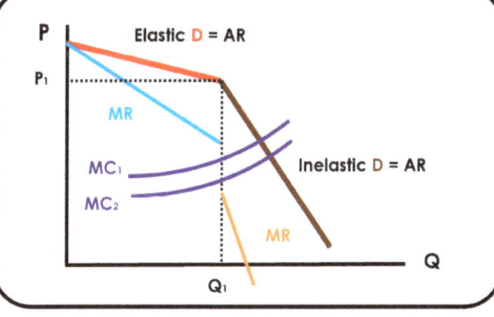

SR = LR

Monopoly

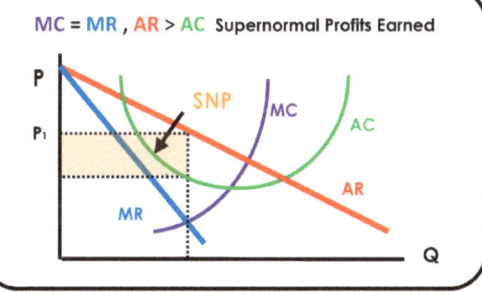

SR = LR

	Perfect Competition	Monopoly	Imperfect Competition	Oligopoly
No *of* **Firms**	Many (all producing identical goods)	One (supplies one good to the entire market)	Many (all producing similar but *not* identical goods)	Small group of firms

13. Perfect Competition

Perfect Competition (PC) is a type of market structure where there are many similar firms producing an identical product in an industry

Many firms with *1 basic product* = the *entire industry*

CHARACTERISTICS

- Many near identical firms provide output at **one fixed market price**
- Many **close substitutes** are available for the **same** product (i.e. potatoes)

ASSUMPTIONS

- Many **buyers** and **sellers** in the market
- **Buyers** and **sellers** act independently of each other
- No **barriers to entry/exit** exist
- **Aim of firms** is to **maximise profits**
- **Many Firms** in Industry
- **Perfect knowledge** exists
- **Product** is homogenous

IMPLICATIONS

- **PC** applies to many agricultural products (**i.e.** potatoes, tea, rubber, coffee or wheat)
- Firms are **price takers**. They *must* sell output at the prevailing market price
- A firm under PC faces a **horizontal demand curve**. It cannot use P to sell more

Short Run (SR) Equilibrium

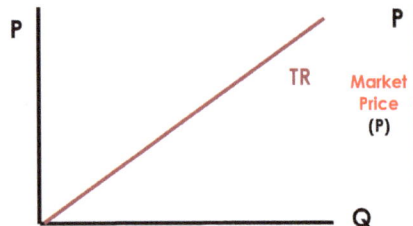

Total Revenue TR
- As price is fixed so TR = **Price** (P) X **Quantity** (Q)
- This is represented by a perfect straight line

- Firm must accept market price (individual firms cant affect market price or quantity)
- Demand curve is a horizontal straight line

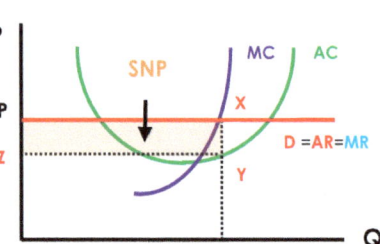

- **MC=MR** (Profit Maximisation)
- Supernormal profits (SNP) being earned (P_1XYZ)
- Not perfectly efficient as firm not operating at lowest point on AC curve

Long Run (LR) Equilibrium

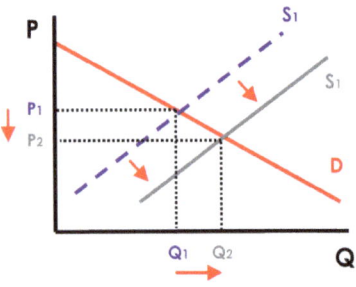

New firms enter due to SNPs Industry Supply↑
$S_1 \rightarrow S_2$

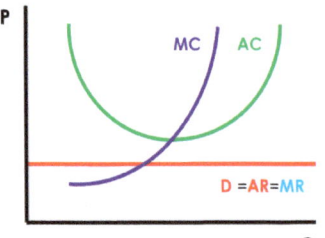

Some firms see the product demand (AR curve) fall sharply. Heavy losses are made as AC > Revenue
Firm will leave industry

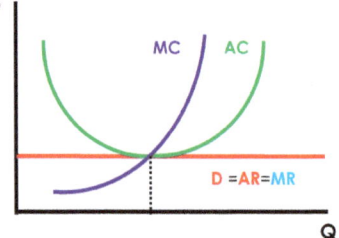

For other firms, new entrants lower AR (Demand) and MR. Costs remain the same. SNPs reduce so that...
AC=AR Normal profits being earned and MC=MR Profit maximisation

14. Imperfect Competition

Imperfect Competition (IC) is a type of market structure between the two extremes of perfect competition **(PC)** and monopoly **(MONO)**

CHARACTERISTICS

- Large number of **independent** firms in industry
- **Aim of firm** is to **maximise profits**
- **Product differentiation** exists. The products are **not homogenous** and **competitive advertising** occurs
- **Free entry/exit** of firms to/from the market
- **Knowledge** is widespread each competitors know **what the other is earning**
- **Many buyers** of the goods produced in the industry

ASSUMPTIONS

- Like in PC, **industry = many buyers and sellers**. Each influences the other
- Widespread knowledge of profit. **High profits (Supernormal Profits or SNPs)** encourage new entrants
- Unlike in PC, products are **not homogenous**. Even if firms similar, consumers distinguish one firm/product from another (branding, packaging, marketing). Firms are **NOT price takers**

Short Run (SR) Equilibrium
At this level of output MC =MR , AR > AC

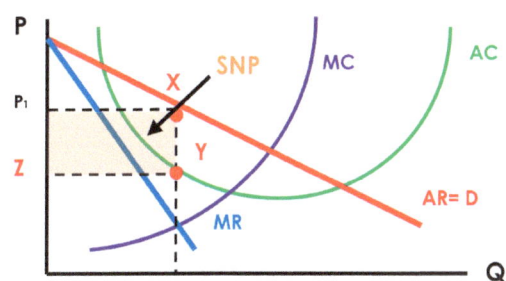

Total supernormal profit **(SNP) = P₁XYZ**

Key Points
1. Demand curve (AR) slopes downward
2. When AR is falling, MR < AR
3. AC is U shaped
4. MC cuts AC at lowest point
5. MC =MR for profit maximisation

In SR, **same as the monopolist (MONO)**
EXCEPT...under imperfect competition, the demand curve is more *elastic* (because of availability of substitutes and more choice between competing companies/products)

Long Run (LR) Equilibrium
New firms enter due to profits (SNPs), forces AR (demand) down.
Prices, output and **profits fall**

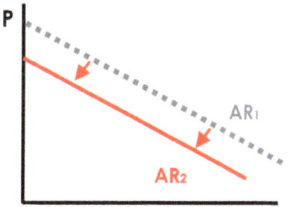

New firms enter due to SNPs (High profits). Existing firms see **demand for their products** fall
AR₁ → AR₂

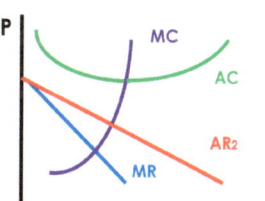

Some firms see the product demand (AR curve) fall sharply. Heavy losses are made as AC > Revenue
Firm will leave industry

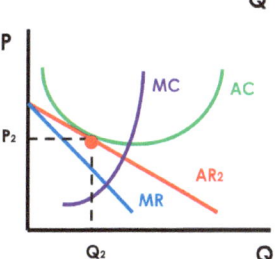

For other firms, new entrants lower AR (Demand) and MR. Costs remain the same. SNPs reduce so that...
AC=AR normal profits being earned
MC=MR profit maximisation

In LR, firm not producing at lowest point on AC curve
Inefficient position

Problems with Imperfect Competition (IC)
Why is IC Inefficient and not PC?

Excess Capacity Producing too little to exploit economies of scale

Competitive Advertising More costs as firms spend to distinguish their products

Why? In IC...
- Some substitutes available
- Firms must innovate, market and brand their products (reduces efficiency)

15. Oligopoly

Oligopoly is a type of market structure where a small number of large firms supply similar products in an industry

CHARACTERISTICS

- Many big similar firms provide industry output but each is aware that **any action on price will provoke a rival to react**
- Many **close substitutes** are available but market is tightly coordinated (with interdependent firms)

ASSUMPTIONS

Dominated Market
- **Few large suppliers** in the industry who have power to influence the sales price
- Industry is '**clustered**' with high concentration ratio (output is concentrated in a handful of big firms)

Price Competition
- Firms reluctant to engage in price competition – want to avoid a price war
- Instead – they engage in **non price competition** i.e. free gifts, promotions, coupons or sponsorship

Barriers to Entry Exist

Sticky Prices
Cyclical periods of price stability and intense price competition

Objectives
Other than max profits

Product Differentiation
Huge amounts spent on advertising to distinguish g/s

Collusion
2+ Firms can collude to restrict competition to increase joint profit

Firms Interdependent
Each decision is 'reaction based' on what rivals may do

The Kinked Demand Curve
Remember, it's a tale of two halves

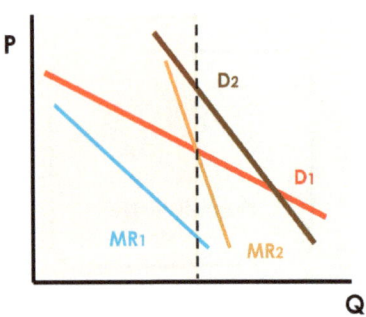

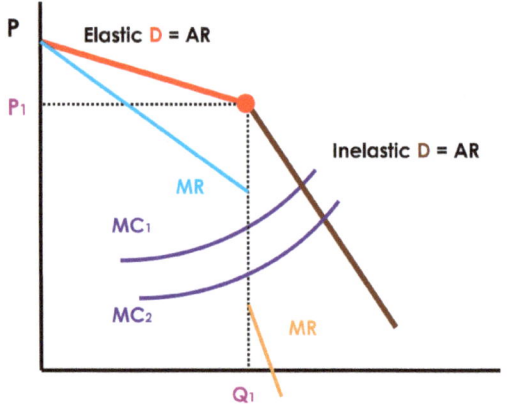

Firms will always aim to keep **profits high** and keep their position in the market (**market share**)

- A firm can *only* do two things: ↓ or ↑P
- Either rivals follow the firm (after ↓P) or don't (after ↑P)
- These two reactions suggest two distinctively different demand (*and therefore* **MR**) curves

  D_1 (MR_1 is twice as steep as D_1)
  D_2 (MR_2 is twice as steep as D_2)

Increase in Price If a firm ↑P (>P_1), it will lose a disproportionate share of the market (customers will switch to rival similar products). An **elastic** demand curve (**AR**) exists (>P_1)

Decrease in Price If a firm ↓P (<P_1), it wont gain many customers – its rivals will likely follow and lower prices (causing a price war). An **inelastic** demand curve (AR) exists (<P_1). So a firm likely wont change its price (price stability)

Why are prices so stable? A firms **marginal cost** (**MC**) can change and not cause the firm to have to change its price (as MR is still equal to MC) – thanks to the vertical MR curve (unique to oligopoly)

ASSUMPTIONS (Continued)

Barriers to Entry
- High **start up costs**
- **Brand proliferation** (several brands advertised and controlled by one large company)
- **Economies of scale** (EOS) in advertising
- **Cost advantages** of existing firms (EOSs, well trained workforce, customer good will/loyalty or patents)

Price Competition
(and Price Leadership)

- **Price Leader:** One firm in dominant position because of large size or early market entry
- This leader may set its prices independently of others in the industry (but a price increase can cause a price war – self defeating)

Collusion
Any action taken by separate and rival companies to restrict competition between them (and increase profits)

2 Types

Explicit Collusion
Separate companies jointly decide to collude
(i.e. via a cartel)

- **Fixed price** applies to all firms
- **Refusal to supply/buy** to/from retailers not in the cartel
- **Quota system which limits products to certain agreed amounts** (to keep price as high as possible)

Implicit (Tacit) Collusion
No formal agreement between firms but each firm recognises that joint profits will be higher if firms behave as monopolists (i.e. OPEC)

- **(Quasi) Fixed price** a firm will not provoke its rivals into a price war
- **Joint policy of profit maximisation** each firm can set MC=MR
- **Conflicting aims** (a) maximise profits (b) cooperate with competitors

Objectives (other than profit maximisation)

Avoid Gov Interference
High profits attract suspicion/ regulation government will impose restrictions to encourage more competition/ tackle monopoly power **Will opt for lower output**

Keep Market Position
High profits attract new entrants (and potential price wars) causing loss of sales. Firm will engage in **'limit pricing' (a certain price level to limit profits)**. Potential firms discouraged from entering

Satisfaction
Small family business will be happy with a certain profit to have a good standard of living. Don't want the stress and added workload of higher output

Fixed Salary
Companies where managers are **not shareholders** (semi-state public companies) do not aim to max profit. They aim to provide a public service (i.e. bus service or postal service) – salary of these managers **fixed regardless of profit**

Baumol's Theory
'Inverse U' Shaped Graph

Once an **established minimum level of profit** reached – firm focuses on other objectives (not concerned with maximising sales, profit or revenue – at the peak of the 'inverse U' curve)

16. Monopoly

Monopoly (MONO) is a type of market structure where there is only one firm producing in an industry

So **1 firm** with **1 product** = the **entire** industry

CHARACTERISTICS

- One firm controls **entire output** of the industry
- No **close substitutes** are available for the **only** product

ASSUMPTIONS

- **1 Firm** in Industry
- **Aim of firm** is to **maximise profits**
- Significant **barriers to entry**
- **Supernormal Profits** can be earned
- Monopolist cant control both P and Q supplied

IMPLICATIONS

- More likely to attract government **(regulator)** monitoring
- **Barriers** mean short run **profit maximising position** is maintained in the long run
- Monopolist faces downward sloping demand curve – It must **lower P** to **sell more**

HOW BARRIERS TO ENTRY ARISE

- **Economies of Scale** — Firm operating so efficiently (and is huge) so no room for competitors + high start up costs for new entrant
- **Trade Agreements** — Companies agree to share market and restrict competition in some way
- **Sole Ownership of Raw Material** — Natural monopoly in production
- **Monopoly due to Patent/ Copyright** — New production method = patent to prevent rival copying patent/processes for period of time (new entrants discouraged)
- **Product Differentiation** — Advertising/marketing can be so successful - customers think no real alternative (i.e iPad)
- **Mergers & Takeovers** — May achieve by taking over competitors/rivals selling similar products
- **Legal Monopoly** — State gives exclusive right to supply a g/s

Short Run (SR) and Long Run (LR) Equilibrium

In order to sell more, a monopolist must **lower price**

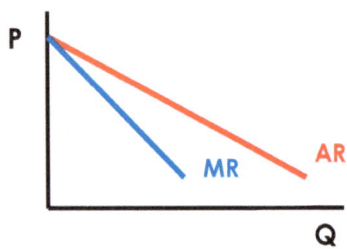

When **price (AR)** is reduced to sell more – **MR** will be less than **P**

AC will be U shaped. MC cuts AC at lowest point (**see #10**). In LR...

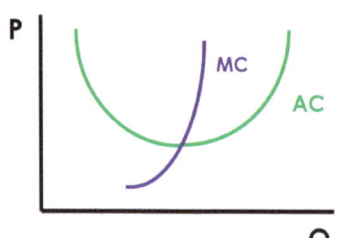

Monopolist will produce where **MC = MR** (Profit Maximisation)

At this output level **MC = MR**, **AR > AC**
Total supernormal profit **(SNP)** = P_1XYZ

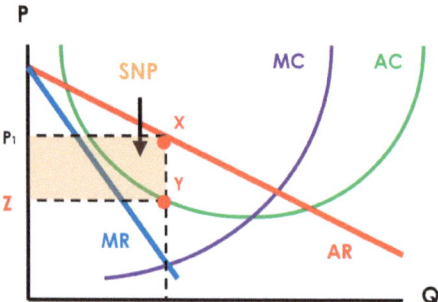

17. Price Discrimination

Selling of a good (or service) to different consumers at different prices, where such prices aren't caused by **differences in cost**

Who does it? **Monopolists (and near Monopolists)!**   Why? **To maximise profits!**

| Selling **SAME** goods to **DIFFERENT** consumers at **DIFFERENT** prices | **2** TYPES | Selling **SAME** goods at different **QUANTITIES** to **SAME** consumers at **DIFFERENT** prices |

How Is it done?

Example: Cinema tickets

| All consumers have different **price elasticities** of **demand (PED)** Cinema charges different prices for the same seat |  | **ELASTIC CUSTOMERS** Those on lower/fixed incomes: retired, students, elderly, unemployed **INELASTIC CUSTOMERS** Higher incomes: teenagers, employed (double income, no kids) | | A price **discriminating monopolist** breaks down the overall market into sub-markets **(depending on these different PEDs)** | → | **Why?** **To maximise profits!** (and revenue) The monopolist will charge each market segment the **highest possible price** |

2 Market Segments Elderly and Standard (Cinema Go-ers)

(A) Elderly (More Elastic) + **(B) Standard** (More Inelastic) = **Total Market**

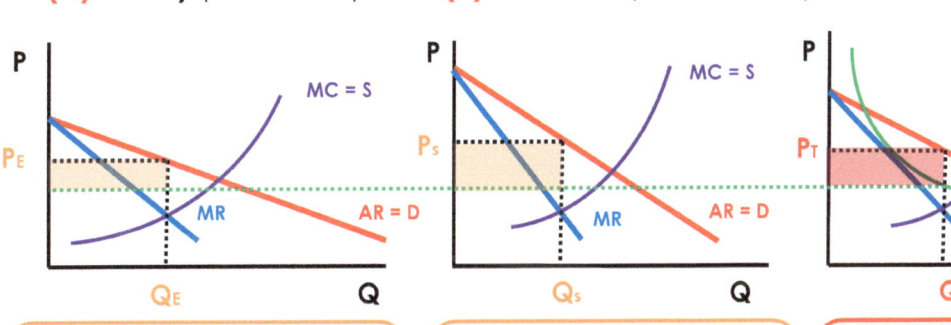

| The elderly are far more responsive to a change in price. P_E **is less** than the standard price P_S and **less** than the average price P_T
• Costs are the same for **all segments**
• Sets **MR=MC** to get max profits | The 'standard' person is less responsive to a change in price. P_S is **more** than the elderly price P_E and **more** than the average price P_T
• Costs are the same for **all segments**
• Set **MR=MC** to max profits | To maximise profits, the monopolist matches **MR=MC** in the total market and **THEN** in each submarket (Costs equal)

Cinema company maximises profits and revenue by adjusting prices so that **MR=MC** in **all segments** |

Conditions Necessary for Price Discrimination

Element of Monopoly Power
Some **barriers to entry must exist** so new entrants can't undercut the price charged by the monopolist

Distinct and Separate Markets
Consumers must **not be able to resell** to each other (i.e. elderly selling cinema ticket to standard customers)

Differing Elasticities of Demand
Price discriminating monopolist will **KNOW** about different PEDs of its customers

Price Characteristics of Consumers

Consumer Ignorance
They must be unaware that a **substitute good is available** from another supplier at lower prices

Consumer Attitude
They must be willing to pay higher price for good supplied by one firm because of a **certain status attached**

Consumer Inertia
They must be reluctant to **change suppliers** should they exist (now or in the future)

18. Markets for the Factors of Production

A certain minimum quantity of each of the **4 factors of production (FOP)** is required to produce any good or service (g/s)

What determines **Demand** for a FOP?

Derived Demand
Factor not wanted for its own sake – it is useful to produce a g/s people want
↑Demand for finished good =
↑Demand for factors needed to make it

Profitability of Return
The firms choice to employ more FOPs depends on the extra (marginal) **output** and **revenue** earned from employing them

Marginal Physical Productivity (MPP)
The **extra output** produced as a result of the employment of an extra unit of FOP i.e. new worker, new machine etc

MPP rises at **low** levels because of **increasing returns to labour**

1. **MPP rises** at first due to **specialisation and division of labour**
2. **MPP** will **fall** eventually due to **law of diminishing returns**

Marginal Revenue Productivity (MRP)
The **extra revenue** produced as a result of the employment of an extra unit of FOP i.e. new worker, new machine etc

If the firm is a price taker (as in Perfect Competition)...

MRP = MPP x Price

A firms MRP curve represents the **firms demand** curve for that factor. **MRP** will **fall** eventually due to **law of diminishing returns**

Why doesn't a firm just set **MRP = Price?**

- **MPP** for one factor is not always = **MPP** of another
- Difficult to measure **MPP**

The Issue of Economic Rent

Payment to a factor of production
- **Land** rent
- **Labour** wages
- **Capital** interest
- **Enterprise** profit

−

Transfer Earnings
Minimum payment necessary to keep FOP in current use (discourage movement to another employment)

=

Economic Rent
Any **surplus** earned by a FOP over and above its **transfer earnings**

How to Control Economic Rent?

Impose A Max Price
(like banker wages in new state owned banks)
But skilled workers in demand can always earn high economic rents

Tax It

Government Reduces/Eliminates it by **increasing FOP supply**

19. Land and Rent

Land is one of the **4 factors of production (FOP)**

Land is anything **from nature** and **used in the production of goods/services**

- **Agricultural land** – Foodstuffs, crops, fruit and veg, animal pasture
- **Rivers, Lakes and Seas** – Fisheries, farming (all natural)
- **Mineral Wealth and Natural Resources** (non renewable)
- **Forests** – Timber for construction (non renewable unless replanted)
- **Atmosphere, Weather and Climate** – Adequate rainfall and sunshine

Economic Characteristics of Land

(A) Fixed in Supply

- Supply **S** cannot be ↑ in response to ↑Demand from **D** to **D₁** (you can't make more land)
- ↑Demand will simply cause an ↑price from **P₁** to **P₂**

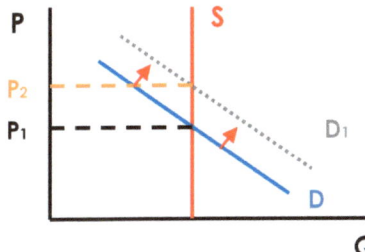

(B) No Cost of Production

- It cost nothing to put land in place (costs only involved in using land). Why?
- Land requires the addition of labour, capital and enterprise
- Land is non-specific – cant be transferred form one use (agricultural) to another (commercial)
- Since land costs nothing, the entire payment to land is economic rent (see #17)

Market Intervention

As land is scarce (and finite), it must be carefully controlled

Local Authorities (Councils) and **planning authorities ensure...**

1. Development takes plan in a planned, responsible and orderly manner
2. Ensure greenbelt/open spaces are preserved and amenities provided to citizens
3. Ensure adequate supply of industrial and commercial sites
4. Ensure areas of historical/special beauty aren't lost to society

20. Labour (and Wages)

Labour is one of the **4 factors of production (FOP)**

Labour is any **manmade effort** which goes into the **production of goods/services**

USUAL DEMAND CURVE
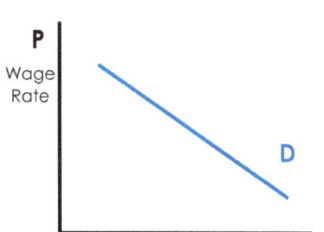

As **Wages↑**, Market Demand for **Labour↓**
- Demand given by the MRP curve of labour
- Employers become less likely to hire due to high cost)

USUAL SUPPLY CURVE
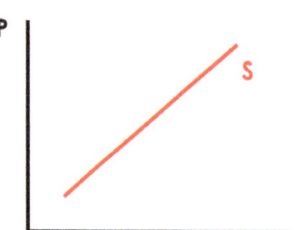

As **Wages↑**, Supply of **Labour↑**
- Higher wages cause more to join labour force (> participation)
- Higher wages mean existing workers work more and are usually more productive (more motivated)

BACKWARD BENDING SUPPLY CURVE

Some Workers Work **Less** as Wages Increase
- Workers prefer more leisure time after wages hit a certain level (given here W_1).
- >W_1 more leisure and less work

DEMAND for Labour

- **Productivity** (Output produced per employee)
- **Availability of Government Subsidies**
- **Demand** for **Company Products**
- **Trade Union Involvement**
- **Taxation on Company Profits**
- **Taxation on Company Employees (PAYE)**
- **Availability of New Technology**

SUPPLY for Labour

- **Population**
  Labour force of an economy = total number of people at work + those looking for work (unemployed)
- **Participation Rate (PR)**
  >PR >Supply
  (*Depends on*: school leaving age, retirement age, job demand and numbers in third level)
- **Hours Worked/Length of Holidays**
  Greater the amount of time spent at work (per employee), the greater the supply of labour

TYPES of UNEMPLOYMENT (UE)

Insufficient Demand for goods/services
Cyclical UE follows boom/bust of economy

Seasonal Unemployment
More employed at different times of the year (Summer, Christmas)

Structural Unemployment
Caused by **change in economy**
1. **Change in pattern of demand** (i.e. decline of shipbuilding in Belfast)
2. **New improved technology**

Fractional Unemployment
(Unavoidable)
- Unemployed between jobs 'lag time'
- Lacking needed skills

Underemployment
Workers not working to full capacity
- Worker employed for only part of week
- Worker employed on a week on-off basis
- Weak productivity (MPP)

How Wages Are Determined

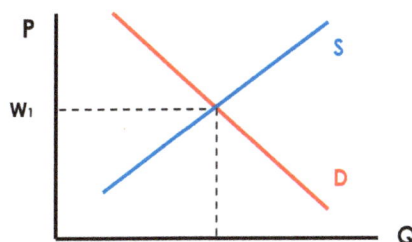

Free Market (No Trade Unions)
- No restrictions on either **demand** or **supply** of labour
- Trade Unions don't restrict **supply**
- Employers doesn't restrict **demand**
- Government doesn't impose a minimum wage

Free Market (With Trade Unions)

Trade Unions (TUs) have **4** effects

1. Set a **minimum wage** below which NO labour will be supplied
2. **Restrict supply** to an occupation to keep wages high (by keeping supply low)
3. **Gov restrictions** temporary wage freezes with unions to control inflation
4. TUs won't accept **wage reductions**

- W₁ minimum wage fixed by trade union
- Q₁ is the quantity of labour employers **willing to employ (demand)** at wage rate W₁
- Q₂ is the quantity of labour workers **willing to supply** (maximum)
- Unemployed = Q₂ - Q₁

End result: Wages kept artificially high (above equilibrium – *see diagram*)

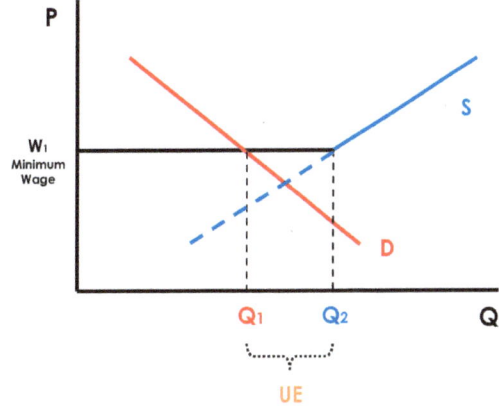

21. Capital (and Interest Rates)

Capital is one of the **4 factors of production (FOP)**

Capital (K) is **anything made by man** and **used in the production** of goods/services

Main Features

1. **K makes labour more productive**
2. **Creation of K involves opportunity cost**
   - Investment requires saving
   - Sacrificing current consumption so future consumption can be higher
3. **Savers provide funds for investors**

Who Saves?
- Those who **incomes exceed current needs**
- Those who decide to **forego present consumption** (in favour of future consumption) i.e. save for a holiday next year

A. **People** don't spend all their income (personal savings)
B. **Companies** don't spend all their profits (retained earnings/dividends)
C. **Government** doesn't spend all its budget surpluses (if available)

SAVERS owners of K who receive a reward (interest)

INVESTORS users of K who pay rewards (interest)

Why Save?
- Buy goods/services in the future
- 'Just in case' rainy day fund
- Retirement income
- Build up credit rating

Factors Affecting Savings = $f(y, Int, I, S, T_S \& G_P)$

y: ↑y ↑Amount saved

Int: ↑Interest Rate ↑Amount saved (> Incentive)

I: If **Inflation Rate > Interest Rate**
Real rate of interest is negative
> Inflation = **Less** incentive to save

S: The **higher** the level of state pension financing, the **lower** level of individual saving for retirement

T$_S$ & G$_P$:
- Gov can ↑↓ tax on interest **(DIRT)**
- Gov can grant tax relief on personal pension plans (encouraging saving)
- Gov can use unique strategies such as Special Savings Incentive Accounts **(SSIA)**

Factors Affecting Rate of Interest

- **Rate charged by ESCB** (European System of Central Banks)
- **Liquidity of Loan**
  > Period of loan = >Rate of interest charged
- **Rate of Inflation**
  > Inflation = > ROI
- **Risk to Lender**
  > Risk = > Rate of Return expected
- **Demand for Loans**
  >Demand >ROI

Factors Affecting Investment

Process of adding to the stock of capital (capital formation)

- **Rate of Interest**
  > ROI = < Willingness to invest
- **Future Demand Expectations**
- **Cost of Capital**
- **Gov Policy**
- **State of Technology**
- **Availability of Skilled Labour Force**

Changes in Interest Rates

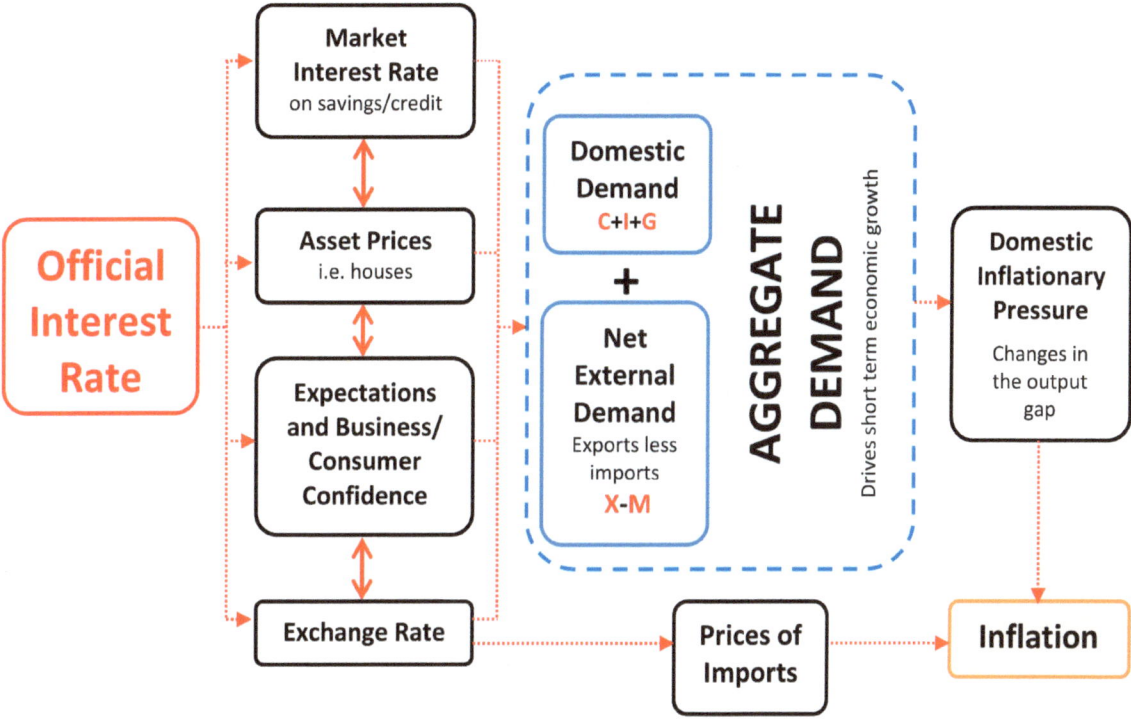

Factors to Consider when setting Interest Rates (IRs)

1. **The Level of Demand (Market Interest Rate):** if consumer spending is too strong, IRs act as automatic stabiliser to control spending to sustainable levels
   - ↑IR = ↑**Savings** and ↓**Demand for Credit** by reducing aggregate demand and raising costs of paying back loans)

2. **Property Prices (Asset Prices):** If there is a likelihood of a housing bubble (helped by cheap mortgage rates and cheap credit), this can raise consumer demand and cause demand pull inflation. For mortgage holders…
   - ↑IR = ↓ **Income/Demand** (Mortgage holders)
   - ↓IR = ↑ **Income/Demand** (Mortgage holders)

3. **Expectations of Business/Consumer Confidence:** the Central Bank will research and assess business/consumer confidence
   - ↑IR = ↓ **Business Expansion/New Businesses**
   - ↓IR = ↑ **Business Expansion/New Businesses**

4. **Exchange Rate Trends:** The value of domestic exports (priced in foreign currency) might be too expensive
   - ↑IR = **Strengthens currency** (↑**Export price**, ↓**competitiveness** and **worsened BOP**)
   - ↓IR = **Weakens currency** (↓**Export price**, ↑**competitiveness** and **strengthened BOP**)

5. **Imported Inflation (Price of Imports)** is the economy dangerously exposed to external factors? This must be quantified and considered

6. **Labour Market:** Is there a likelihood of causing a wage-price spiral (and pricing domestic workers competitively out of the market

Why People **Prefer Liquid Wealth**
(Having readily available **cash** or easily **saleable assets** on hand)

TRANSACTIONS MOTIVE (D_T)

- People need cash for **day to day** spending
- This depends on **income**
- As $Y\uparrow$ $D_T\uparrow$
- R.O.Interest (ROI) has **no** effect on this spending

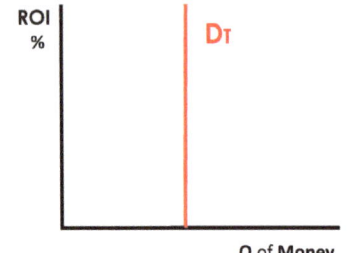

PRECAUTIONARY MOTIVE (D_P)

- Money held in case of emergencies i.e. illness, car repairs etc
- As $Y\uparrow$ $D_P\uparrow$
- ROI has **some** effect (as ROI$\uparrow$, $D_P\downarrow$)

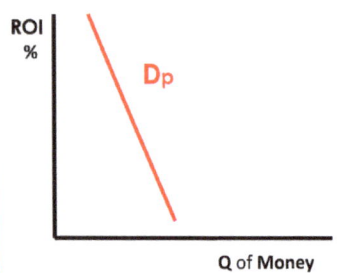

SPECULATIVE MOTIVE (D_S)

- People taking advantage of profit making opportunities
- Investors expect price to rise in the future (so buy now)
- As $Y\uparrow$ $D_S\uparrow$
- ROI has a **big** effect (as ROI$\uparrow$, $D_P\downarrow$)

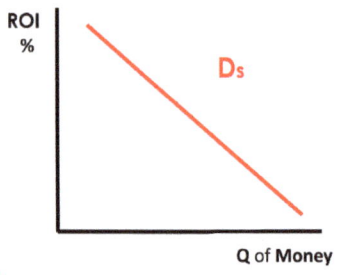

Keynes' Theory of Liquidity Preference

D_M = Aggregate demand (**Precautionary demand D_P + Speculative demand D_S**)

- ROI will be determined by intersection of D_M and S_M

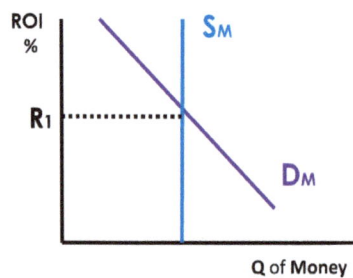

Capital Categories

Capital Widening
Increase in use of K which leaves ratio of capital (K) to labour (L) unchanged

- Factory has 100 workers and 10 machines
- Demand $\uparrow$
- Firm takes on 30 extra workers and 3 machines
- Ratio of K: L before **(1:10) same** as after **(1:10)**

Capital Deepening
Increase in use of K which increases ratio of capital (K) to labour (L)

- Factory has 100 workers and 10 machines
- Demand $\uparrow$
- Firm takes on 10 extra workers and 5 machines
- Ratio of K: L before **(1:10)** different to after **(1:6.6)** – Production now **more** K intensive

22. Enterprise (and Profit)

Enterprise is one of the **4 factors of production (FOP)**

Enterprise **Initiative** involved in **organising land, labour and capital** and which bares the **risks** involved

For **Enterprise** and its practitioner the **'Entrepreneur'** – its all about **RISK**

Types of Risk

Insurable
- **Damage** to infrastructure/property by acts of nature
- **Theft**
- **Dishonesty** by employees (Fidelity insurance)
- **Accidents** to workers or the public
- **Non-Payment** for goods (Breach of contracts)

Non-Insurable
- **Strikes**
- Declining **competitiveness**
- **Competition** from others
- **Loss of profitability**
- Change in **consumer tastes**
- Change in **company leadership**

The Role of Profits in a Free Market System

- **Encourage Risk Taking**
- **Sign of Efficiency**
- **Guide Resources** to their **Most Efficient Use**
- **Encourage Entrepreneurs** to **begin a new business**
- **Encourage a Firm** to **Stay in Business**
- **Ensure Investment** is put to **Best Use**

The Economic Characteristics of Profit

- **Payment to Enterprise is Residual** — Remainder after all other payments of the other FOPs are paid
- **Only FOP capable of a negative reward** (Loss)
- **Return to the Entrepreneur fluctuates more than the other FOPs**

23. Money and Banking

'What is money?' Money is anything that is used to buy/sell goods and services. Money (including credit) is the fuel to the economy

Before money, there was bartering…

Swapping of good(s) for another

Very inefficient/costly. Why?

- **Relies on double coincidence of wants** What you want to buy must be accompanied with what someone wants to sell and vice versa
- **Relative value of goods** How do you quantify and worth?
- **Stops specialisation and division of labour**

So What Defines Money?
Functions of Money

Medium of Exchange
Aid the process exchanging goods/services between people

Measure of Value
Provides a common value where relative values can be compared

Store of Wealth
Allows people to save wealth for the future by depositing it and gaining interest

Means of Payment
Allows for efficient buying/selling (no back and forth as with bartering)

Different Types of Money

Commodity Money
Good whose value serves as value of money i.e. gold coins

Fiat Money
Good whose physical value is less than the value It represents i.e. paper money

Bank Money
Credit created by banks extended to customers via loans, cheques and credit cards

How do Banks Create Credit?

Reserve Ratio (RR)
This 10% is the bank 'reserve ratio' i.e. what % it keeps in reserve

What Determines RR?
- Availability of **creditworthy** customers
- Central bank **monetary policy**
- The state of the **economy**
- The **liquidity** requirements of the bank
- The **solvency** of the bank

Commercial Banks
- Accept cash from depositors
- Depositors only ever demand a small proportion back to use (around **10%**)
- Bank can use the **90%** to **loan out on credit** (keeping enough cash (10%) to meet customers demands)

Commercial Banks can borrow money from the

Central Bank

Credit Creation
Banks can create credit in the economy this way

↑ **Money Supply** =

↑ **Cash Deposits** $\times \dfrac{1}{\text{Reserve Ratio}}$

> Money Supply
- ↑Consumer spending + Boost **aggregate demand** (and **employment**)
- But could ↑**Inflation** and **imports** (worsen balance of trade)

Remember!
- For the eurozone-17, these functions are carried out by the **European Central Bank** (ECB) under European Monetary Union (EMU)
- Each member country within EMU maintains a Central Bank with **limited functions**
- Within EMU – a country lacks the ability change its 'Interest/Exchange Rate' and 'Supply/Print Money'

Functions of the Central Bank

Government Banker
Holds public monies (tax revenue)

Loans
Make loans to commercial (high-street) banks

Reserves
Hold gold and foreign exchange reserves

Research
Carry out economic research and make projections

Interest/Currency Rate
Adjusting interest rates and currency exchange rates (Monetary policy *or* MP)

Supply Money
Issues notes/coin and 'prints money' by issuing credit

Commercial Bank Assets

Bank assets are in two broad categories: **profitable** (normally over the long term) and **liquid** (short term assets readily converted into cash at short notice)

Liquid (SR)

1. **Cash**
2. **Money at call** Money loaned on the interbank market (loaned between banks)
3. **Exchequer Bills (aka Bills of Exchange)** Gov 'loans' out bonds to be repaid with interest after a given time

Profitable (LR)

1. **Government bonds (aka Gilt edged securities)** 'Sold' to debtors at a given rate of interest to be repaid over 3, 5 or 10 years
2. **Term loans (+ Overdrafts)**

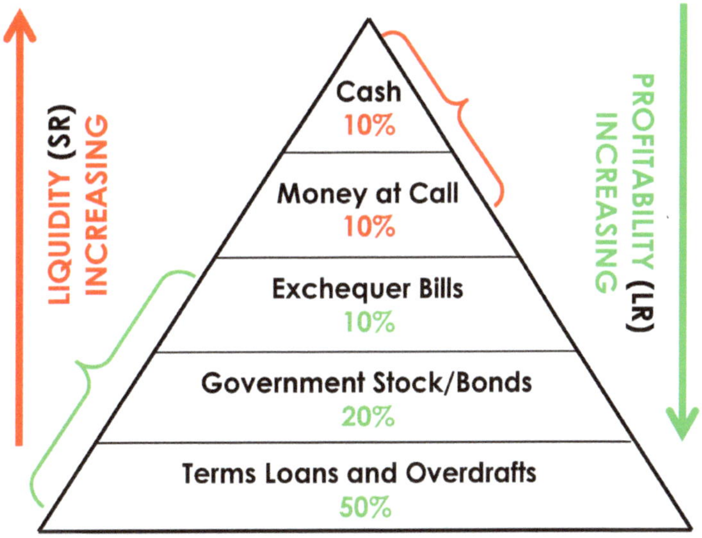

LIQUIDITY (SR) INCREASING
Cash
10%
Money at Call
10%
Exchequer Bills
10%
Government Stock/Bonds
20%
Terms Loans and Overdrafts
50%
PROFITABILITY (LR) INCREASING

Banks Borrow From Each Other

(Interbank Market)

- Major source of **short term financing** for banks
- Banks lends funds to each other and an interbank Interest rate is paid
- If more money is available on the interbank market than is demanded, there is a **surplus.** The interbank interest rate will fall (because demand is insufficient) making lending cheaper

24. Measurement of National Income

National Income = Total Income earned by permanent residents of a country in one year. It is *also* the total value of the flow of goods and services (output) produced over the year (or…the combined spend on this production)

The level of national income can be measured in **3 ways**
Measuring aggregate (1) incomes (2) output or (3) expenditure in the economy

The INCOME Method
The sum of all (factor) incomes

People earn their incomes by supplying FOPs in return for rewards

Rewards: Land (Rent), Labour (Wages), Capital (Interest) and Enterprise (Profit)

National Income (at factor cost) = net *domestic* (from home) product at factor cost + net factor income from non-domestic (from abroad)

Included
All factor incomes generated via production of goods/services

Wages + Rent + Profit (Private Sector businesses) = GDP (by factor income)

Excluded
- **Transfer Payments** i.e. social welfare (dole) payments, state pension etc
- **Private Money Transfers**
- **The Black 'Shadow' Economy** unrecorded income from unofficial sources (criminal)

The OUTPUT Method
The sum of the combined value added of production

Net Domestic Product at factor cost
ADD Depreciation
= Gross Domestic Product at factor cost
ADD Taxes on expenditure
MINUS Subsidies
= Gross Domestic Product at market prices
ADD Net factor income from ROW
= Gross National Product at market prices

GNP = GDP + NFIA
(Using Ireland as an example)

- **GNP** (Gross National Product) = the product of the 'nation' i.e. the GNP of Ireland **includes** the final value of output/expenditure of all Irish owned FOPs at home and abroad
- **GDP** (Gross Domestic Product) = measure of output/expenditure within Irelands borders regardless of company nationality (and where their profits go!)
- **NFIA** (Net Factor Income from Abroad) = That earned (profits) Irish citizens MINUS that earned (profits) by foreigners in Ireland

For Ireland, GDP is higher than GNP (because NFI is negative)

EXPENDITURE Method
Total expenditure on goods and services (aggregate demand)

Gross National Product at market prices
MINUS Taxes on expenditure
ADD Subsidies
= Gross National Product at factor cost
MINUS Depreciation
= Net National Product at factor cost

Sum of Spending
(at current market prices)

$$Y = C + I + G + (X-M)$$

Consumption **(C)**
+ Investment **(I)**
+ Government Spending **(G)**
+ Exports **(X)**
- Imports **(M)**

Uses and Limitations of National Income Figures

Why is it important to measure national income?

1. Make international comparisons
2. Analyse the standard of living
3. Analyse changes in distribution of income between income groups
4. Assist government in policy decisions

Limitations

- Distribution of Income might **mask inequalities**

- Figures Wont Explain **level of Government Involvement** in Economy

- No Account Taken of **Nature of Goods**

- Using GDP stats to measure standard of living **overly simplistic**

- **Fails to take account of Population**
  >Pop >GDP

- GDP figures **don't show human development standards** i.e. life expectancy, adult literacy, education attainment etc

25. Factors Affecting National Income

Potential level of national income (Y): Max level of output an economy is capable of producing given its resources

This isn't constant…it depends on **quality of the FOPs** and the **skill/flexibility of the workforce**

Actual Level of National Income Depends on…

$$Y = C + I + G + X - M$$

Income — Consumption — Investment — Government Spending — Exports — Imports

Exports − Imports = Trade Balance

C

With your income (Y), you either consume/spend it (C) or you save it (S)

$$Y = C + S$$

What encourages you to spend rather than save?
1. How much you earn
2. The Interest rate
3. Availability of credit facilities

I

Spending by businesses on capital equipment (to replace or add to existing stock)

What encourages you to invest?
1. Expectations
2. The interest rate
3. Availability of credit facilities
4. Return on capital employed

G

Depends on **government resources** (if a government is facing austerity in public expenditure, there won't be much money left to pay for expanding/increasing public expenditure)

X

Depend on **strength of demand for your production abroad**

What makes your exports desirable?
1. Advantageous exchange rate
2. Quality of exports (i.e. Irish beef)
3. Type of exports (what you're selling)

M

Depends on **private sector needs** which **depends on growth** (and **income!**)

↑ Y (Income) ↑Imports as ↑Economic Growth/Output

The **Circular Flow** of **Income**

Shows how **different sectors of the macro-economy are** linked

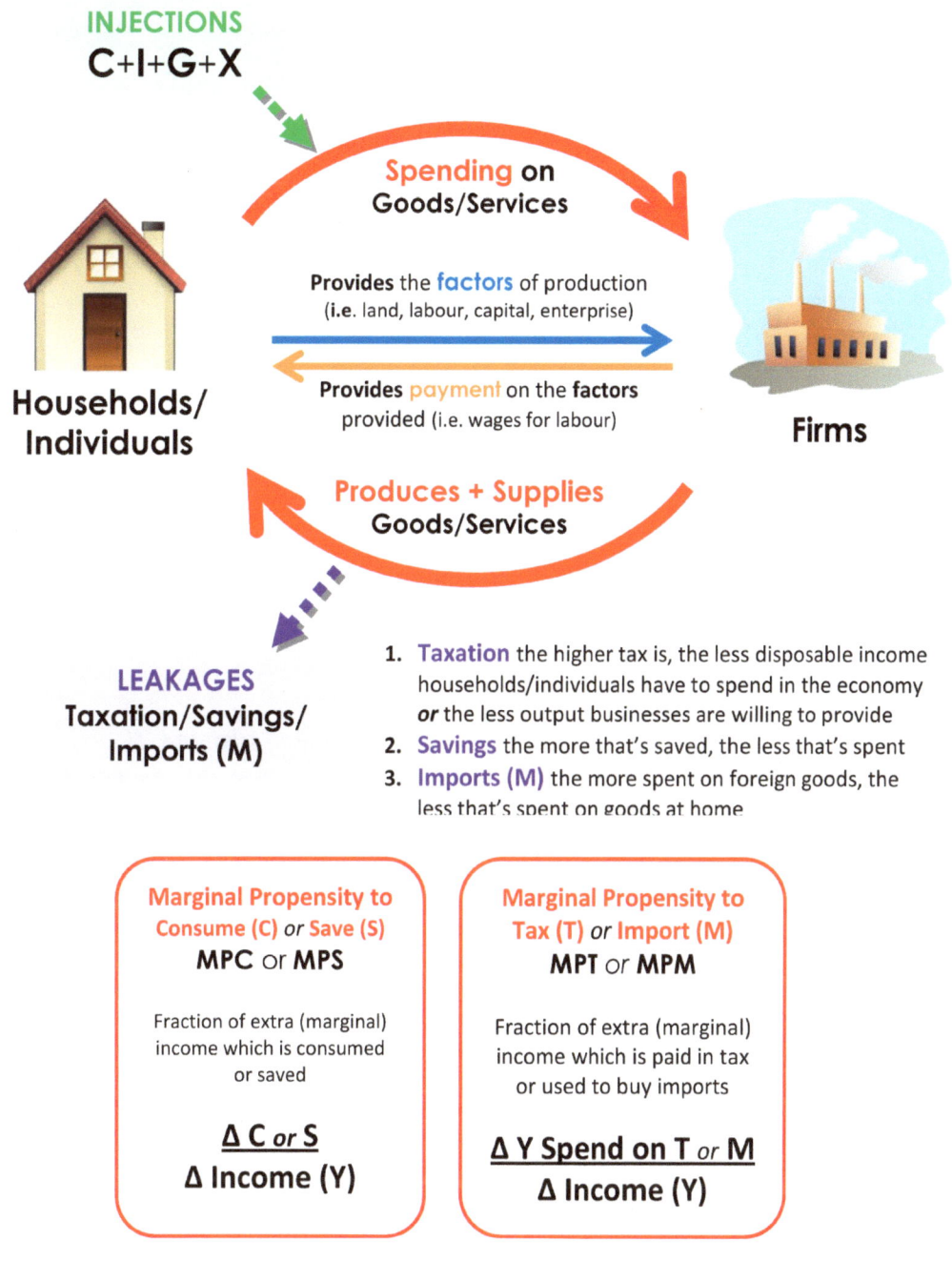

INJECTIONS
C+I+G+X

Spending on Goods/Services

Provides the **factors** of production (**i.e.** land, labour, capital, enterprise)

Provides payment on the **factors** provided (i.e. wages for labour)

Households/Individuals

Firms

Produces + Supplies Goods/Services

LEAKAGES
Taxation/Savings/Imports (M)

1. **Taxation** the higher tax is, the less disposable income households/individuals have to spend in the economy *or* the less output businesses are willing to provide
2. **Savings** the more that's saved, the less that's spent
3. **Imports (M)** the more spent on foreign goods, the less that's spent on goods at home

Marginal Propensity to Consume (C) *or* **Save (S)**
MPC *or* MPS

Fraction of extra (marginal) income which is consumed or saved

$$\frac{\Delta C \text{ or } S}{\Delta \text{ Income (Y)}}$$

Marginal Propensity to Tax (T) *or* **Import (M)**
MPT *or* MPM

Fraction of extra (marginal) income which is paid in tax or used to buy imports

$$\frac{\Delta Y \text{ Spend on T } or \text{ M}}{\Delta \text{ Income (Y)}}$$

MULTIPLIER
Number of times an **injection** results in an ↑Y

$$\frac{1}{\text{MPS + MPM + MPT}} \times \text{Injection}$$

26. The Price Level (and Inflation)

Inflation is the rate of a gradual rise in the general level of prices. If the rate of inflation exceeds income growth, the purchasing power of consumers falls

How Price Changes are Measured

A Simple Price Index

1. Choose **base years** i.e 2009, '10 **base year = 100**
2. Find **price of goods** in 2011
3. Express price today as a % of price in the base year

$$\frac{\text{Current Price}}{\text{Old Price}} \times \frac{100}{1} = \text{SI}$$

Year	2009	2010	2011
Simple Index	100	SI$_1$	SI$_2$

A Composite (Weighted) Price Index

Each good is given a 'weight' according to the % of income spend on it (i.e. its importance in consumer expenditure)

1. Choose **base year** i.e. 2007
2. **Decide** which goods to include
3. Find **price of goods** today (Y)
4. Calculate **simple price index**

Year	Good A	Good B	Good C
2009	100	100	100
2010	SI(A)	SI(B)	SI(C)
2011	SI(A)	SI(B)	SI(C)

5. **Find weights** (% of income spent on each goods) i.e. 20% of income spent on **Good A** means the Simple Index for A SI(A) Is multiplied by 20. 45% is spent on **Good B**, 35% on **Good C**.
6. Calculate **Weighted Average (WA)**

Year	Good A	Good B	Good C
2009	100 x 20	100 x45	100 x 35
2010	SI(A) x 20	SI(B) x 45	SI(C) x 35
2011	SI(A) x 20	SI(B) x 45	SI(C) x 35

7. Add all 3 values from each year together and divide by 100. Result is our **Composite Price Index!**

Year	Total	Composite Index
2009	10,000	100.00
2010	WA (All Goods)	WA ÷ 100
2011	WA (All Goods)	WA ÷ 100

The Consumer Price Index

- Most common example of a composite (weighted) price index
- Measures change in the average level of prices paid for consumer goods/services by all private individuals in the country

KEY LIMITATIONS

- **Based on Average Spending Patterns** Doesn't relate to cost/standard of living changes
- **Weights Apply in Base Year Only** Fraction of income should change!
- **New Products not included**
- **Improvement in Features of Goods Ignored**
- **Switch to Cheaper Brands** Not Measured

USES OF THE CPI

- To Measure Inflation Rate
- Provide Justification for Widening Tax Bands
- Maintaining real value of welfare payments
- Wage Negotiations (Maintaining real value of incomes)
- Maintaining real value of savings
- Indexation of Investments Avoid Underinsurance

Causes (and Types) of Inflation?

Demand-Pull Inflation

When the economy cant produce enough to meet demand

Demand > Supply

Caused By:
- Low interest rates
- High economic growth
- Producer unable to meet demand for goods (so they can ↑**Profits** by ↑**Price**)
- In smaller economies, excess demand means ↑**Imports** (worsening balance of trade)

Government Induced Inflation

Government policy can cause inflation

Caused By:
1. Gov ↑ **Direct/Indirect Taxes**
   - Reduces economic activity
   - Taxes on inputs increase cost to manufacturers which is passed on (Cost-Push Inflation)
2. Gov ↑ **Public Expenditure**
3. **Loose Banking Policy** (low regulation of banks)
   - Gov allows banks dole too many loans (overheat economy)

Cost-Push Inflation

When prices rise because producers face greater cost of production (COP)

How does COP rise?
1. ↑**Price** of imported raw materials (**Imported Inflation**)
2. ↑**Cost of Labour** – wage increases = pressure on profit margins = ↑Prices to compensate (**Wage-Price Spiral**)
3. ↑**Price** of home produced raw materials (component costs)

Both Can Be Classed
'**Demand-Pull Inflation**'

Economic Effects of Inflation

Production Encouraged
↑P = ↑Qs

Consumption Encouraged
If consumers expected Inflation to continue

Fixed Incomes Lose Out
Includes employers, welfare recipients and pensioners

Self Employed Gain
They ↑P > Inflation

Borrowers Gain/Lenders Lose
(If Inflation rate > Interest rate)
- Borrowers pay **less** (in real terms)
- For lenders, value of savings held **falls**

Loss of International Competitiveness
Exports can become too expensive on world markets (**less** desirable, demand **falls**...state **loses** income)

Government Benefits
- **Gov Borrowing:** If Inflation rate > Interest rate, real government borrowing level **falls**
- **Gov Revenue:** inflation brings more people into tax net (gradually, as incomes rise and rates are static)

27. Economic Objectives of the Government

All elected governments have common key economic goals to achieve during their term in office

The Economic Objectives of Governments

Provision of Adequate Infrastructure
- **Communication networks** (high speed broadband access)
- **Transport networks** (motorways, national roads, waterways and airports)
- **Public services** (post offices, water, sewerage, electricity)

Equilibrium on Balance of Payments
- Ideally, gov aims to achieve **Imports = Exports** (at least)
- If **imports>exports** – country living beyond its means (buying too many foreign goods)
- If **exports>imports** – good sign but inflation can happen

Achievement of Economic Growth
Growing output is vital

Balanced Regional Development
Spread development via national development plans

Control of Inflation
(Price Stability)
- Control of prices is very important. Inflation erodes economic competitiveness
- > Inflation >Cost of your exports on foreign markets
- **Inflation** = Bad for countries reputation

Achievement of Full Employment
- Situation where jobs are available for all those willing to work at existing wage levels
- Full employment = control of unemployment

Control of Public Expenditure
Keep costs and revenues balanced

Instruments of Government Economic Policy

Fiscal Policy
Control of **government revenue** and **expenditure**
How?
↑↓ Tax or
↓↑ Spending

Monetary Policy
Control of **the level of money in the economy**
How?
↑↓ Interest Rate   or
↓↑ Money Supply

Exchange Rate Policy
Control of **the value of your currency**
How?
Devaluation (worth less)
Revaluation (worth more)

Direct Intervention
Gov **intervenes**
(+ Keynesianism)
How?
State companies/spending
State laws
Capital/Public projects

Conflicts Between Government Objectives

Full Employment (FE) Vs. Price Stability/ Control of Inflation
FE means ↑public expenditure in the economy which can ↑ inflation

Economic Growth (EG) Vs. Balanced Regional Development
EG means growing investment + output (private and public). **Balanced development** = state imposes **taxes** on high income earners to ↑social welfare (discouraging investment)

Full Employment (FE) Vs. Control of Spending
FE means ↑public expenditure + budget deficits which can ↑ inflation + national debt

28. Fiscal Policy

Fiscal Policy: Any action by government which affects the size or composition of government revenue or expenditure

Key Fiscal Terms

Current Expenditure
Spending on day to day items financing the 'running of the country' i.e. public sector wages, cost of running government departments

Current Revenue
Money received by the government in taxation and other income

Capital Expenditure
Spending on long term projects such as large scale infrastructure

Exchequer Balance
Sum of current and capital budgets

Budgets

Current Budget Deficit
[Expenditure > Revenue]
Caused By
- Weak economic growth (high unemployment)
- External economic shocks

Current Budget Surplus
[Revenue > Expenditure]
Caused By
- Strong economic growth (and high employment/spending)
- Strong tax revenue

Neutral Budget
Revenue = Expenditure
Aka Balanced Budget

ADDS to... / ADDS to... → **NATIONAL DEBT**
REDUCES the.. / REDUCES the.. →
NO EFFECT on... / NO EFFECT on... →

NATIONAL DEBT
The total outstanding debt owed by government

It's a bad thing as/if it...

- **Pushes up Interest rates** (In a small economy with small savings supply)
- Is spent to finance **current spending** rather than **investment** (country is living beyond its means)
- **Crowds out private sector** (increases state involvement in the economy)
- **Causes higher taxation** (Higher borrowing is ultimately unsustainable and will reduce aggregate demand and economic growth)
- As national debt grows, so do **interest payments**. In a downturn (as since 2007) these payments are difficult to make and the public budget gets cut, causing hardship (welfare, education, transport services)

It's a good thing if...

- Its spent on **infrastructure** (if money borrowed in spent on productive or social projects to provide necessary public services or increase economic output)
- Its spend on **'self liquidating uses'** (if money is medium term and will likely be repaid eventually i.e. current spending on banks)
- Its due to **natural growth** in the economy
- It leads to **borrowing at home**, instead of abroad (which can recoups tax)

Characteristics of the Good Tax System

Equity — Should be based on ability to pay

Certainty — Know your tax liability

Economy — Cost of collection must be low

Automatic Stabiliser — Should have stabling effect on national income level

Convenience — Must be easy to collect tax

Redistribution — Taxation should enable to redistribute wealth from rich to poor

Flexible — Changeable to suit economic conditions

Not Discourage Work or Investment

Types of Taxation

DIRECT
Income Tax
Corporation Tax
Capital Gains Tax
Capital Acquisitions Tax

Advantages
- Based on principle of **equity, certainty** and **economy**
- **Convenient** to taxpayer
- Acts as **automatic stabiliser**

Disadvantages
- As it rises, work is **discouraged** (**absenteeism** becomes a problem)
- **Tax evasion** rises
- Can discourage **investment**

INDIRECT
VAT
Excise Duties
Custom Duties
Stamp Duties

Advantages
- **Cost of collection** is low (Economy)
- Easier to **extract** from the public (less sensitive)
- Doesn't **discourage work**
- Acts as **automatic stabiliser**

Disadvantages
- Inflationary/Deflationary
- Not **equitable**
- Hard to **predict yield** (based on assumptions of consumer spending)

29. International Trade

CHARACTERISTICS

Wider Choice — Countries can consume products they don't produce domestically

↑Competition — Lower prices for consumer (and higher efficiencies) where producers compete

↑Productivity — Allows economy to Produce more efficiently. Better use of scarce resources (exploit comparative advantage), technology, innovation and 'best practice' ideas

↑ Standard of Living (SOL)
- **Individual** worker gains by specialisation of labour
- **Country** is able to enjoy a higher SOL by concentrating on what its good at

Improved Relations — > Contact with outside world and neighbours

Provides Markets For **Excess Output**

BASIS

Absolute Advantage

One country can produce a good cheaper than others

	Chemicals	Coal
Ireland	1000	2000
UK	500	3000

Law of Absolute Advantage
Each country should specialise in producing a good in which is has an **absolute advantage**

Comparative Advantage

One country is relatively more efficient producing a both goods **(output per worker)**

	Beer	Bread
Ireland	50	80
Denmark	100	90

Compared with 'Beer', Ireland produces 'Bread' at a much closer level to the Danish level than 'Beer'

Law of Comparative Advantage
(Aka **Ricardo's Theory**)

Each country should specialise in producing a good at which it is *relatively most* efficient (and fulfil its other requirements through trade)

- Why would Country **A** differ to **B**? Different **'endowments' (available quantities)** of key **factors of production (FOPs)** [aka Heckscher-Ohlin Theory]
- This maximises **economic welfare** (through specialisation of what you're good at doing)

How Valid is this Law/Theory?

- Ignores **Transport Costs**
- Assumes **Free Trade Exists**
- Assumes **Constant Returns to Scale**
- Assumes FOPs (i.e. Labour) Will **Move Across Occupations**
- Assumes **Specialisation can occur unhindered**

What determines Comparative Advantage
(i.e. cost of production)

- **Factor Endowments** (and their quality)
- Investment in **R&D**
- Tariffs/Quotas
- Long Term **Inflation Rate**
- **Exchange Rate** Changes

Summary: What is Free Trade?

Exchange — Buy what they cant produce cheaply/efficiently at home

Specialisation — Exploit economies of scale

The Government and Free Trade

Why Government Intervenes

- Protect from **competition by low wage countries**
- Protect an **'Infant Industry' from competition**
- To prevent **'Dumping'** of low price goods (from Asia)
- To protect **domestic workers** (in domestic industries)
- For **political purposes** i.e. US embargo of Cuba

How a Government Intervenes

1. **Tariffs**
   - Tariffs **increase** the price of an imported good (after it arrives). This can be ad valorem (% of selling price) or a specific 'duty' amount
   - **Earn** revenue
   - **Reduce** level of imports (depending on elasticity of demand)

2. **Quotas**
   - Physical **limit** placed by government on the import limit of a good
   - Raises **no** revenue
   - **Limits** market size

3. **Exchange Control**
   - Imports are **limited** to a certain money value (in foreign currency)

4. **Embargoes**
   - Complete **ban** on the importation of certain goods
   - **Political/Health and safety** reasons

5. **Administrative Barriers**
   - "Red Tape" **obstacles** for importers i.e. excessive documentation, length processing delays

6. **Subsidies**
   - Provide **incentives** to exporting firms to **encourage exports** i.e. grants, low interest loans, marketing assistance

30. Currencies and Exchange Rates

One of the most commonly items of trade is currency. Investors come in many forms, from the average tourist buying a different currency before a holiday to giant pension and hedge funds who profit from speculating on the rising/falling prices of currencies

The price of a currency is relative – it is measured in relation to the price of another currency, rather than itself

Why Does the Price of a Currency Change?

You often hear on the news 'the dollar has fallen in value against the euro..' **What does this mean?**

On **Monday:** €1 = $1
On **Tuesday:** €1 = $0.75

The main reasons for this:

1. **The economy.** If one economy using a certain currency appears to be weakening, then the price of the currency falls as demand falls
2. **Profitability:** investors will always aim to maxmise their return. If a country has high interest rates, government bonds (debt) and other investments will have a much greater return than countries with low interest rates. Investors will buy from the high interest rate economy, demand will soar and the value of the currency will rise.

Two Main Exchange Regimes

Floating

Governments via their Central Banks adjust the exchange rates to suit economic policies or in response to market perceptions (or to maintain harmonious trade relations)

Commonplace today especially in developed economies

Pegged/Fixed

Countries 'peg' or ride a stronger, respected and stable currency to build credibility, reduce instability and promote investment in their economies. Many European currencies pegged to the US$ after WW2 to rebuild their economies

Originally, many countries fixed their currencies to the value of gold (a fixed value) in a regime known as the Gold Standard

More common in the 19th and 20th centuries

Demand for a Currency

The Q_D (Quantity Demanded) of your currency in the 'foreign exchange market' depends on **3 factors**

1. The **current exchange rate**
2. The **expected exchange rate**
3. The **interest rate** (at home and abroad)

Current Exchange Rate (CER)

>CER = <Q_D of your currency

- **High exchange rate** = More expensive exports = Less Desirable/Low Demand for goods = Low Demand for stuff priced in your currency (exports)
- **Low exchange rate** = High expectation of profits by currency investors (they expect the currency to get dearer so they buy now)

Expected Exchange Rate (EER)

>EER = >Q_D of your currency

Investors expect currency to get dearer so they buy now to sell at profit later

The Interest Rate (IR)

>IR = >Q_D of your currency (and your assets)

Higher interest rate = Higher rate of return (so investors buy more of assets priced in your currency)

Expected Exchange Rate (EER)

>EER = <Qs of your currency

Investors expect currency to get dearer. Those who hold your home currency will hold it to sell later (for profit then)

The Interest Rate (IR)

>IR = <Qs of your currency (and your assets)

Higher interest rate = Higher rate of return (so investors buy more of assets priced in your currency and supply is snapped up)

Current Exchange Rate (CER)

>CER = >Qs of your currency

- **High exchange rate** = Cheaper imports = Buying more foreign currency (using your home currency)
- **High exchange rate** = High expectation of losses by holding your home currency (so, you will dump your home currency and buy more profitable currencies)

Supply of a Currency

The **Qs** (Quantity Supplied) of your currency in the 'foreign exchange market' depends on **3 factors**

1. The **current** exchange rate
2. The **expected** exchange rate
3. The **interest rate** (at home and abroad)

Pros and Cons of a Strong Currency

Pros

- **Cheaper imports** = higher standards of living for citizens (import cheaper consumer goods/cheaper food) = More disposable income
- **Low inflation** by disciplining domestic producers and domestic wage demands (as your trade competitiveness erodes)
- Low inflation = Less upward pressure on **Interest rates**

Cons

- **Erosion in trade competitiveness** worsens **trade balance** (citizens import more and buy less at home)
- Weakness of exports reduces **economic growth** (domestic economy shrinks)
- Domestic demand and domestic industry suffers (**upward pressure on unemployment**)
- Mounting deficits bad for **investor confidence**

31. The Balance of Payments

The **Balance of Payments (BOP)** is a record of all the financial transactions that are made between all those active in the domestic economy (consumers, businesses and the government) and the rest of the world

Includes

- How much is being spent by domestic consumers/businesses on **imports**
- Composed of **2 parts**
  1. **Current Account**
  2. **Capital Account**
- The **level of exports** are (production sold abroad to foreign countries)

CURRENT ACCOUNT
All flows of money received from the purchase of goods/services

Visible Balance (of Trade) = **Exports** (Goods) − **Imports** (Goods)

Invisible Balance = **Exports** (Services) − **Imports** (Services)

Exports (Services) Examples
- Earnings of domestic airlines from foreign passengers
- Earnings of domestic hotels from foreign guests
- Earnings of domestic singers/bands from abroad
- Subsidies received domestically from the EU
- Earnings of Irish consultancies from foreign clients

Imports (Services) Examples
- Your own citizens using foreign airlines
- Spending by your own citizens on holidays abroad
- Payments by your own citizens to foreign companies
- Earnings of foreign artists in your country
- Taxes pay by your country to the EU
- All interest pay on debt owed to those abroad

Net Investment Income
Interest payments, profits and dividends from external assets owned by nationals but sited abroad

Current Transfers
Private transfers between countries and government transfers (to EU, UN and other international bodes)

= **Net Balance on Current Account**

Visible Balance + **Invisible Balance** + **Net Investment Income** + **Current Transfers**

CAPITAL ACCOUNT
All flows associated with 'capital' items i.e. private capital, official capital and banking

Private Capital Transactions
Purchases of land, factory buildings or company shares

+

Official Capital Transactions
Government borrowing and the sale of government stock/bonds to foreigners by the government

+

Banking Transactions
Change in net external position of banks

= **Total Capital Transactions**

Net Balance on Current Account
+
Total Capital Transactions

= **BOP on Capital/Current Account**

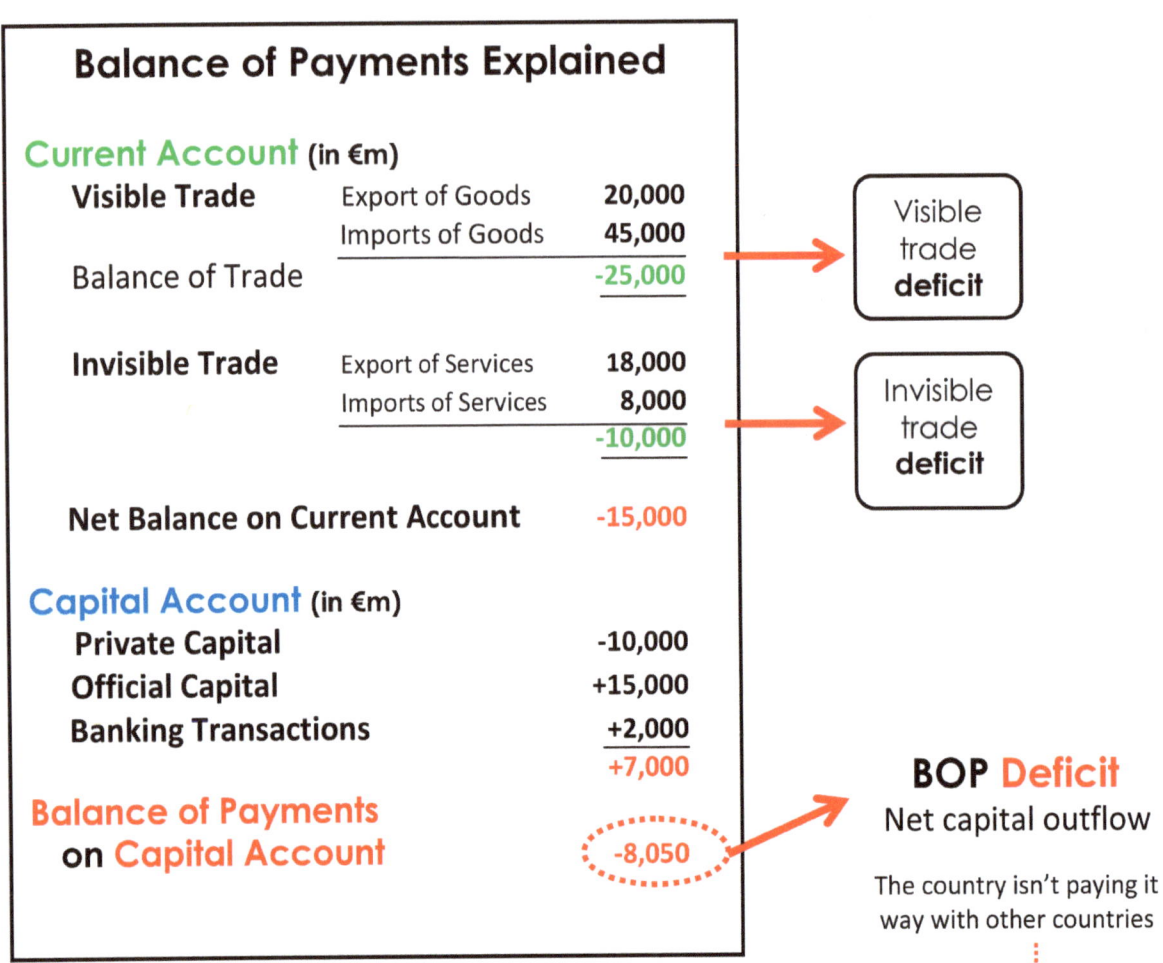

Balance of Payments Explained

Current Account (in €m)

Visible Trade	Export of Goods	20,000
	Imports of Goods	45,000
Balance of Trade		-25,000
Invisible Trade	Export of Services	18,000
	Imports of Services	8,000
		-10,000
Net Balance on Current Account		-15,000

→ Visible trade **deficit**

→ Invisible trade **deficit**

Capital Account (in €m)

Private Capital	-10,000
Official Capital	+15,000
Banking Transactions	+2,000
	+7,000
Balance of Payments on Capital Account	-8,050

BOP Deficit
Net capital outflow

The country isn't paying it way with other countries

Why is there a BOP (Trade) Deficit?

SHORT TERM FACTORS

1. **Booming home economy** means high consumer demand which can't be satisfied by domestic production. Imports grow
2. **Strong exchange rate** reduces prices of imports, switching consumer spending away from domestic production (cheaper to import)
3. **Global economic weakness** damages export growth

MEDIUM/LONG TERM FACTORS

1. **Structural problems** in the economy (long term decline of once strong exporting sectors i.e. deindustrialisation and the growth of more competitive and footloose services)
2. **Decline in comparative advantage** in the international economy
3. Low level of **capital investment**
4. **Productivity/Competitiveness** problems

Many economies in Western Europe are shifting toward INVISIBLE exports (services) rather than VISIBLE exports (goods)

- Economies are exposed to increased competition in services
- This exposes them more to investor confidence (fluctuates)
- Employment shifts to service based (most 'developed' economies = **70%**)

32. The Evolution of the International Economic System

The International Monetary Fund (IMF)

- Intergovernmental organisation HQ'ed in Washington D.C.
- Set up by as part of the post-war Bretton Woods Agreement of **1944** in New Hampshire, USA
- Commenced operations in **1947**
- It has **187 members** (nations)

The World Bank
(Fmr. International Bank for Reconstruction and Development)

- Intergovernmental organisation
- Each member contributes on proportion to their share in world trade
- Set up by as part of the post-war Bretton Woods Agreement of **1944** in New Hampshire, USA
- Commenced operations in **1946**
- It has **187 members** (nations)

Goals

1. Encourage **monetary cooperation**
2. Promote **expansion** of world trade
3. **Stabilise exchange rates** (by linking every member currency to the US$)
4. Facilitate a **system of payments** between countries (for Marshall Aid)
5. Provide funds (and advice) or countries in **BOP crises** (and stop devaluations though it now advocates it as a first step to fiscal rectitude)

Goals

Facilitate loans to member governments for development (poorly developing countries) and reconstruction (all)

Consists of **2 Organisations**

1. **International Finance Corporation** (IFC): Invests in private capital projects via loans and guarantees
2. **International Development Association** (IDA): Gives long term loans at very low rates for infrastructural development

The General Agreements on Tariffs and Trade (GATT)

- HQ'ed in Geneva, Switzerland
- In operation **1947-1993**. Replaced by WTO **1995-**
- Consists of several 'rounds' of agreements including the **Kennedy Round**. Most recent is the **Doha Round (2001-)**
- It has **153 members** (nations)

The World Trade Organisation (WTO)

Goals

1. Promote **free and unhindered trade**
2. Provide **forum for negotiations** and for **dispute resolution**
3. Increase **multilateral trade** (combating protectionism)
4. Reduce **tariffs** and **quotas**
5. Abolish and penalise **preferential trade agreements** which distort trade
6. **Help the developing world** to compete on the world market (in agriculture)

33. Economic Development and Growth

Development: The Increase in output per person, involving a signfiicant **change (evolution) in society**
Growth: Increase in output **without change in society**

Rostow's 5 Stages of Economic Growth

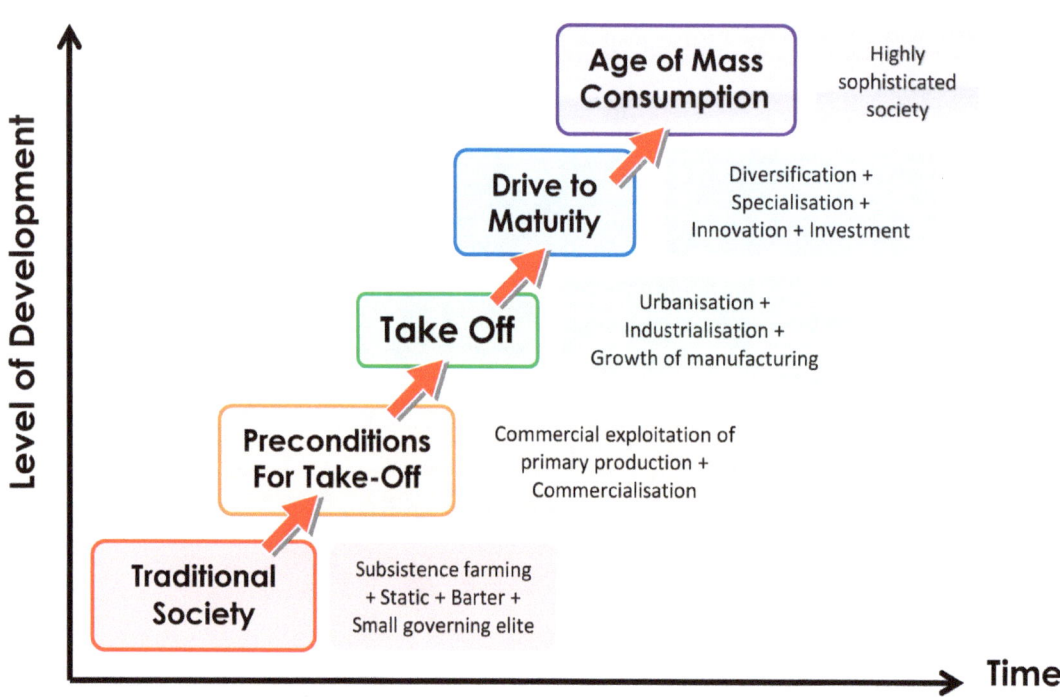

Traditional Society	Society is **very primitive** with **very limited technology** and a reliance on **subsistence farming**. People rely on community bartering rather than advanced coinage/banking. Society is governed by a small wealthy **ruling elite** with strong traditional values
Preconditions For Take-Off	Citizens see possibilities of improvement. Growing **specialisation** and **commercialisation** of skills and **investment in infrastructure**. Increasing focus on **exports** (of primary production such as mining and farming) and fuelling investment through surpluses
Take Off	Economic growth becomes **self sustaining**. Huge technological advancement = development of domestic manufacturing sector. Agriculture output/worker increases as do services. **Urban flight + rural depopulation** skyrockets (regional city growth). Political modernisation = growing democratisation (demands). Greater pending on education and social development
Drive to Maturity	Range of **domestic production** widens – country replaces imports with domestic production (**import substitution**). Increasing **diversification** and **investment** (from home and abroad). Increasing need for innovation for efficiency gains in existing techniques
Age of Mass Consumption	Economy becomes heavily geared toward **service provision** (consumer orientation) due to exploiting comparative advantages in trade. High quality world class **infrastructure** is now in existence. Citizenry demand **consumer durable goods**

Rostow's 5 Stages of Economic Growth (Summary Table)

	Economic Growth	Society	Polity	Tech/Innovation	Industry	Investment
Traditional Society	-	Traditional Community values	Small hierarchical governing elite	Limited technology	Mainly agricultural (subsistence farming)	Very low if any (Barter economy)
Pre-Take Off	Low (focus on export of agriculture)	Aspirational citizenry (eager to follow success of neighbour)	Increasing elite legitimacy problems	Increasing commercialisation	Enhanced agri-productivity Start of low level manufacturing (focus on extractive industry i.e. mining)	Surplus from agricultural exports used (funding expansion of domestic markets)
Take Off	High (and sophisticated)	High level of social change (urbanised + educated society) Growth of wealthy 'social' elite	Increasing demands for democracy (led by dominant intellectual leaders)	New productive methods introduced High level of entrepreneurship	Industrialisation (helped by new infrastructure + manufacturing growth + social change)	Indigenous spending + Aid from abroad (on new infrastructure)
Maturity	High (Spread throughout society)	Strong urbanised society (Fuelling social discontent)	Political revolutions then modern political institutions	High (extract efficiency from existing tech – high degree of professionalism)	High level of Import substitution (natural endowments strong) Growth of new industries	High level of Indigenous spending + Foreign investors
Mass Consumption	Low to High	Bureaucratic society driven by consumer durables	Competitive democracy	High	Mainly services ('Third Wave' of industrial growth)	Indigenous spending + Foreign investors

Least Developed Countries (LDCs)

CHARACTERISTICS

- Low Income Per Head
- High % Engaged in Agriculture
- Poor Terms of Trade
- Poor Living Conditions
- Rapid Population Growth
- Uneven Wealth Distribution
- Lack of Resources for Investment
- Low Adult Literacy

STRATEGIES FOR DEVELOPMENT

Self Sufficiency
Fulfil domestic needs/wants via growing the domestic economy
India

Trickle Down Policy
Placing few restrictions on industry/low taxes on wealthy to promote business growth and employment
Brazil

Export-Led Growth
Country concentrates on mass production of cheap, reliance consumer goods i.e. toys
Many South-east Asian economies

Central Planning
State planning and public ownership of the means of production
Cuba

WHATS NEEDED FOR DEVELOPMENT?

- Foreign Aid
- Capital
- Infrastructural Improvements
- Greater Openness to trade (and ideas)
- Increased agricultural output
- Peace and Political Stability
- ↑Literacy (and Education)

Economic Growth

Benefits

- **Greater standard of living** with wider consumer choice of goods/services
- Greater output = **Higher employment** levels (and enhanced demand for other FOPs)
- **Reduces poverty levels** (increasing employment and more resources to pay for social welfare)
- Provides resources for **capital/infrastructural spending** and **public expenditure** on education, transport and health

Costs

- Uneven distribution of wealth causing widening **income inequality**
- **Damage to environment**
- Urbanisation leading to **ghettoisation in cities** (poverty/crime black spots) and **rural depopulation**
- Uneven growth can cause **unbalanced regional development**

34. The Economics of Population

Demography is the study of **population**

Key Stats in Demography

Birth Rate — Average annual number of live births per 1,000 people

Fertility Rate — Average annual number of children born to a woman of childbearing years

Death Rate — Average annual number of deaths per 1,000 people

Density of Population — Average number of people per square kilometre

Infant Mortality Rate — Average number of infant deaths per 1,000 live births

Developing Countries (LDCs)
1. **HIGH** birth rate
2. **HIGH** fertility rate
3. **HIGH** death rate
4. **LOW** population density (usually rural societies)
5. **HIGH** infant mortality rate

Developed Countries
1. **LOW** birth rate
2. **LOW** fertility rate
3. **LOW** death rate
4. **HIGH** population density (more urbanised societies)
5. **LOW** infant mortality rate

Population Movements

Emigration — GOING OUT — Residents leaving their home country (in search of employment, better prospects or other reasons)

+

Immigration — COMING IN — Foreign nationals entering the home country (in search of employment, better prospects or other reasons)

=

Migration — TOTAL CHANGE — The difference between those who leave (emigration) and those who arrive (immigration)

Economic Effects of Emigration

1. **Falling demand** for domestic goods and services
2. **Reduced demand for imports** (Improves country's balance of payments situation)
3. **'Brain drain'** as highly skilled/college graduates leave (despite free state education at home)
4. Pressure on **home companies to raise pay and conditions** to prevent their employees leaving
5. **'Pressure valve'** for unemployment – reducing it
6. High rates = **Symbolic of an economy in crisis** (Negative on national pride)

Pull Factors
Conditions in other countries which makes working and living there more attractive

- Higher pay
- Better social life/cultural experiences
- Training and development opportunities
- Better job prospects
- Booming economy

Push Factors
Conditions in the home country which cause residents to leave

- Low (or falling) pay
- Religious/social reasons
- Poor training and development opportunities
- Poor job prospects
- Economic recession

35. History of Economic Thought

Mercantilism

Arguments **in favour of state involvement** in society

- Based on **'Bullionism'** Economic health of a nation measured stores of gold/silver in reserve
- Link between **wealth and trade** – As Exports> Imports = Building up gold/silver reserves (prosperity)
- Trade only where it benefits your exports. Ignore **principle of comparative advantage**
- Gov should **reduce imports** via tariffs, subsidies and granting exclusive rights (National advantage and imperative to run a trade surplus i.e. money gold/silver must flow in)
- **Import substitution/Economic self sufficiency** vital (via domestic manufacturing
- **Strong political authority** vital (at the expense of individual liberty) to coordinate economy and solve conflict
- State would **aggressively seek to expand its position** as with great wealth comes great political power
- **Key Industry:** Manufacturing (but agriculture needs to be encouraged)
- **Colonies should be exploited** as a source of raw materials and a market for manufactured goods

16th and 17th Century

Physiocrats

'Government of nature'. Rely on 'rule of nature' **not state involvement.** Maximum freedom of the individual

François Quesnay

- Allow economy to follow **'natural order'**
- Role of state is to **uphold 'natural order'** and **preserve private property**
- **Key Industry:** Agriculture (all wealth derives from the soil)
- **3 Economic Sectors**
  1. **Proprietary Class** (Landowners)
  2. **Productive Class** (Agri Labourers)
  3. **Sterile Class** (Artisans and Merchants)
- **Free trade with no protectionism** – 'Laissez faire' (leave it alone)

18th Century

Classical School (Capitalism)

Rely on 'rule of nature' **not state involvement.** Maximum freedom of the individual. Labour is the source of value (**Labour Theory of Value**) + **Profit Motive**

Adam Smith

- **Major Work:** 'The Wealth of Nations' **(1776)**
- Advanced **'laissez faire'** system of natural liberty + **specialisation** of ones labour (new Political/Social order)
- Everyone should be free to pursue own **'self interest'** + **Free International trade**
- **Trade = Zero Sum** (Everyone gains!)
- Selfish interests benefits society as, unobstructed by **government**, the **'invisible hand'** of markets will guide markets to their most efficient uses and determine prices
- **State role:** national defence, legal system, public works (via taxation)

Thomas Malthus

- **Major Work:** Pessimistic work 'Essay on the Principle of Population.' **(1798)**
- **Population growth** = Geometric growth but **food supply growth** = Arithmetic growth (poverty and starvation is inevitable)
- This leads to a low standard of living for all (fueled by **'Iron Law of Wages'** i.e ↑Wages → Population ↓SOL ↓Wages)
- Only checks on pop growth 'misery', 'vice' and 'moral restraint'

David Ricardo

- **Major Work:** 'Principles of Political Economy and Taxation' **(1817)**
- Pessimistic 'Theory on Rent': Small population (POP) = supply food domestically via best land + low rent = High output/Profits
- **Demand for land↑, Wages↑, POP↑,** Demand for food↑, Rents↑, Landowning Profits↑
- Bad thing for industrial productivity
- Also, **Theory of Comparative Advantage** in Trade

John Baptiste Say

- **Major Work:** 'Treatise on Political Economy' **(1803)**
- **Law of Markets (Says Law)** = Supply creates its own demand
- People work to buy goods/services (demand) and exchange their **own surplus goods for the surplus goods of others.** So, no overproduction! **Income can be saved, Interest rates** would fall, **demand** would rise

JS Mill

- **Major Work:** 'Principles of Political Society' **(1848)**
- **State role:** Gov can tax excess earnings (landowners) and wealth spread
- **Overproduction is impossible** (Says Law)
- **Increasing returns to scale** for large scale firms
- **Trade unions** have a role in countering employer power
- Accepted **subsistence theory of wages** (Iron Law)

18th and 19th Century

TIME

TIME

19th Century

Socialism

Much social and political change (after Industrial Revolution and Railway Mania of mid 1800s)

Karl Marx

- **Major Work:** Communist Manifesto (1848)
- **Labour Theory of Value** (like Classical writers) : **Value of a good** = Labour needed to produce it
- **No invisible hand**
- Capitalists exploit wealth (created by Labour)
- Capitalists want ↑ **Profit** so they demand more Labour, ↑ **Wages** (above subsistence)
- Capitalists don't want to pay ↑ **Wages** (hits profitability)
- Replace workers with technology, new methods of production (less labour intensive) = Unemployment
- In the drive for ↑ **Profit, Wages** eventually ↓
- But **only Labour can generate profits.** Unemployment = Reduced demand (Vicious cycle)
- Workers become 'deskilled' as mere 'cogs in a machine' for profit (**Alienated**)
- Provokes **profitable firms to merge** – centralised power in fewer and fewer capitalists
- Poverty, oppression, exploitation and enslavement ensues

Early/Mid 20th Century

Rebirth of Classical School
(Neo-Classical)

The '**Paradox of Value**': How do we judge the value of a good?

- Smith, Marx and Ricardo all believed in the **Labour Theory of Value** (it's the cost of labour that determines price of a good). If its easy to produce, it will be cheap.
- Birth of a **new idea**:
  Marginal Utility (of consuming additional units) determines price. High MU = High Price

(Neo Classical) Keynesianism

Lessons of 1930s Great Depression

Recessions a major problem. Says Law wrong? Unemployment can persist because wages can remain high. Interest rates can be ineffective to spur economic growth

John Maynard Keynes

- **Major Work:** The General Theory of Employment, Interest and Money (**1936**)
- **Idea:** Damage Management
- **Unemployment** is caused by insufficient demand for goods/services in the economy and the economy can settle with high unemployment for a long period. Afterall 'in the Long Run, we're all dead' so action needs to be short run
- **Wages aren't always flexible downwards** (can't be cut – provokes industrial/social unrest') aka '**Sticky Wages**'
- **Level of investment** in economy (in recession) **insufficient.** Supply > Demand and unemployment follows
- **Fiscal Policy** of a state can prevent unemployment and economic recession
- **State plays a role** (**regulates the economy when needed**) raise aggregate demand itself by stimulus spending (by borrowing and investing i.e. by running budget deficits **IF** it means coming the economy healthy)
- This creates **employment** (and **prevents unemployment**)
- State spending smooths out the bumps caused by market cycle (**Boom-Bust**)

Late 20th Century

Monetarism

Monetary Policy *not* Fiscal Policy should be key to economic management (Keynesianism doesn't help with inflation)

Milton Freidman

- ↑ **Money Supply** = ↑ **Inflation** (↓ **Competitiveness** of exports)...so...increasing public spending will only increase prices (not output)
- **Control Money Supply** (via interest rates, limiting loans and public spending) = **Control inflation**
- **Idea:** Supply side policies (anything that attempts to influence labour supply or supply of goods and services)
  1. Cut income tax
  2. Encourage market competition
  3. Reduce role of trade unions in the labour market
- **Minimise state role in economy** return to laissez faire (back to Smith's 'invisible hand') via privatisation of state assets and encouraging business growth
- **Price stability MOST important goal** (not full employment as in Keynesianism)